DECLUTTER

YOUR MIND

How to Stop Overthinking, Beat Your Inner Critic, and Reframe Your Negative Thoughts with Healthy Habits

TIFFANY ADAMS

Copyright 2019 © Tiffany Adams

All rights reserved.

No part of this guide may be reproduced in any form without permission in writing from the publisher except in the case of review.

Legal & Disclaimer

This book is copyright protected. It is only for personal use. You cannot amend, distribute, sell, use, quote or paraphrase any part, or the content within this book, without the consent of the author or publisher.

Please note the information contained within this document is for educational and entertainment purposes only. All effort has been executed to present accurate, up to date, reliable, complete information. No warranties of any kind are declared or implied. Readers acknowledge that the author is not engaging in the rendering of legal, financial, medical or professional advice. The content within this book has been derived from various sources. Please consult a licensed professional before attempting any techniques outlined in this book.

By reading this document, the reader agrees that under no circumstances is the author responsible for any losses, direct or indirect, that are incurred as a result of the use of information contained within this document, including, but not limited to, errors, omissions, or inaccuracies.

Table of Contents

Introduction

Scientists and researchers have been studying the brain for years but still have concluded little about the wholeness of what our minds represent. Our brains are the master of everything we do and think about, starting when we are children just introduced to the world. The things we experience, how we learn, and our perceptions and beliefs are all stored by our brain. Think of it as a computer system—when you receive a brand new phone or computer, it has nothing stored on it to start. As you open more web pages and download more applications, the computer's memory stores these processes. Our brains are the same, except they don't store webpages or applications; instead, they store memories of our lives. Based on how we think and what we do throughout our lifetimes, different things can be stored inside the brain's storage and data. This process is amazing; however, over time, our minds can become cluttered because it doesn't file certain life experiences in their proper places, promoting stress and panic. This occurrence is called **mental clutter**.

The problem is that we rely on our brains for everything and trust that it will do its job. We constantly depend on our brains to file memories appropriately, memorize important dates and names, and remind us about deadlines we cannot miss. When we rely on our brains to bring these memories to the surface when we need them, we also ask a lot from it, considering the brain is already responsible for so many other functions such as physical movements, sending hormones across the body, and compartmentalizing and separating good thoughts from the bad. We take for granted what our minds do and expect so much from it without ever giving it a break. Even when we sleep, our brains are actively processing everything that has happened during the day, including our past events and future worries, in the form of dreams. But what if there was a way to give it a break by decluttering our minds for more productivity and clearing the way for true clarity and success?

In this straightforward handbook, you will learn how to declutter your mind so you can live a life with clarity and potential. You will define the triggers that weigh you down and identify the reasons you feel so worn out and tired all the time. Among learning what can clutter your mind like toxic people and surroundings, you will realize how you can fix these obstacles to suit your needs. Most of what causes a cluttered mind is believing we are busy, or we have toxic habits that we are unaware of. In the first chapter, you will get to understand the causes of negative thinking and be able to identify where your overthinking and worries stem from. Do you feel as though other people or influential circumstances are standing in your way? Do you feel overwhelmed and under pressure when it comes time to focus? Do you feel bogged down and mentally unsatisfied, and just prefer to go to sleep? Truthfully, the only thing that stands in your way is yourself and guess what—you have the power to fix it all.

Between the negative self-talk, the cruel inner critic, the excessive worries, the pressure of social media and society, and the never-ending tasks you feel you *must* do, it's no wonder you have become your own worst enemy. Throughout this book, you will learn how to overcome the deep pressures of the universe, beat your inner critic, and become a more self-loving and confident individual. Most of your issues come from deep-structured habits and patterns that you have followed almost all your life. Are you ready to change all that? Are you prepared to commit to being a better you? And do you want to learn and challenge all the ways you can become decluttered mentally, physically, and emotionally? Then you have come to the right place. However, don't think by reading this book that all your dreams will come true—they won't unless you dedicate yourself and put the work and effort in to change. It all starts with a choice, and that choice is up to you.

By the end of this book, I promise you will have a more productive perspective, know what you want and how to get it, and have a more organized inbox both digitally and mentally. Rewiring your brain requires effort, work, and motivation which is what this book will ultimately test to see if you are ready. You must be ready if you are tired of feeling exhausted from the stress you have been taking on. Have you wished for the opportunity to grow? Does your life feel too busy for you to be bothered to make any modifications? This book will change your mind, and it only takes five minutes of your time each day to gain a different perspective. Imagine that—by learning these decluttering techniques, you will fight your depression, break out of your shell, and ultimately learn how to control your mind without it ever controlling you again.

You deserve happiness. You deserve to love yourself. You deserve to take care of your internal spirit. You deserve forgiveness and gratitude. You deserve to be the best version of yourself. So, why not start now?

Chapter One: Understanding Mental Clutter — Where Does it Come From?

Mental clutter is the term used by many scientific experts as *having too much going on in your mind*. It is the chatter of your inner critic and the stimuli your brain is taking in from all around you. This mental clutter can cause serious problems for you and your health and could be why you have felt so drained. Are your days usually spent worrying and obsessing over things to the point of insanity? Are you having a difficult time staying positive? If you answered yes, then it probably means your mind is overwhelmed with stimuli. Work, school, relationships, tasks, shopping, and other big life events can become too intense for your brain. People who suffer from disorders such as anxiety, depression, ADHD, obsessive-compulsive disorder, and PTSD are usually the most at risk for a cluttered mind.[1] If you don't learn how to **declutter** your mind and take a breather from your stress, the

---

[1] Smith, E.-M. (n.d.). *What is Negative Thinking? How It Destroys Your Mental Health.* [online] Available at: https://www.healthyplace.com/self-help/positivity/what-is-negative-thinking-how-it-destroys-your-mental-health

condition can get worse and result in permanent negativity and a dissociative disorder. Are you already negative 90% of the time? Then it means it may be time to find the root of the problem and declutter your mind. It makes sense that even *"healthy"* people experience mental clutter from our evolving world of technology and endless tasks of to-dos. So, what could be the causes?

Sometimes the issue is that you are used to putting things you feel don't matter aside.[2] You may think you will forget about them over time, but your brain has not. Other times the issue is the many decisions to make in your life, and then you continuously question yourself on the paths that lie in front of you. Overthinking and listening to your inner critic results from putting off deciding and problem-solving, ultimately causing more mental clutter. Just these two

---

[2] Desy, P. (2019). *Three Causes of Mental Clutter*. [online] Available at: https://www.learnreligions.com/causes-of-mental-clutter-1729494

theories alone can lag your brain because the issues are running through your subconscious constantly. When avoided for too long, stress takes over, causing anxiety, depression, and perfectionism with unimportant tasks.[3] You may need to take a mental vacation. The fact is that if you avoid essential matters throughout the day, you can lose sleep at night. When this loss happens, it's because the minute you have any *quiet time*, your brain kicks into overdrive. To fix this unhealthy pattern, you must understand your inner critic and what is triggering your mental fog. Other causes include listening to your negative thoughts too often, procrastinating, feeling guilty for your failures, and avoiding the problem rather than dealing with it.

---

[3] Smith, E.-M. (n.d.). *What is Negative Thinking? How It Destroys Your Mental Health.* [online] Available at: https://www.healthyplace.com/self-help/positivity/what-is-negative-thinking-how-it-destroys-your-mental-health

Basically, mental clutter revolves around:[4]

- A negative thought pattern of "should I or shouldn't I?" and "What if xxx?"
- Trouble letting go of the past or a wrong decision
- Unfinished tasks such as sending important emails, replying to your voicemail, paying bills, etc.
- Endless worry over things you cannot control
- Low self-esteem leading to perfectionism and second-guessing yourself
- Criticizing yourself when you don't meet your perfect expectations.

So, what can you do about it? We can start by learning the core triggers.

---

[4] Best, J. (2018). *Mental Clutter*. [online] Available at: https://www.apdo.co.uk/mental-clutter/

Decrease the Inner Critic's Noise Level

Mental noise is what I call the inner critic. It's the voice inside your head that criticizes you, bullies you, and continually says you're never good enough. This is one cause of mental clutter. Inner critics are the core to negative thinking and come out when it is most quiet and when there are very few distractions around you. Most people avoid their thoughts and try to distract themselves from hushing their voices. It never works as the voice comes back stronger later and dictates most of your decisions. The best thing to do is to listen to what your inner critic is telling you, then challenge it and ask it questions like **why**, **what**, and **how**.

Procrastination

Procrastination means to either avoid or prolong a task that must be done. When something needs to be done, such as sorting through the bills or working on a presentation, some people avoid it by working on other things. That way, they can feel better about procrastinating because they can use the other task as an excuse. But, just because you are busy doing other things does not mean that the distractions are more important than the task you are avoiding. At first, you may procrastinate the small tasks, but over time, avoiding everyday tasks while accomplishing the smaller ones will eventually cause you to neglect the more significant projects. What you may not realize through this process is that your brain stores every job you have, which causes clutter the longer you put those tasks off. The best thing to do is *not* procrastinate. You will feel much better when the task is complete, and you will waste less time.

Avoidance Catching Up to You

Much like procrastination and wasting time, avoiding the task does not mean that the task isn't avoiding you; it catches up to you through your inner critic. For example, say you borrowed money from someone a while ago. A few months go by, and every time you receive a paycheck, your brain sends a reminder you owe someone money. You then convince yourself that they probably aren't expecting it. The person may have told you to take your time, so you said to yourself that there are other essential things you should buy at that moment. Another month goes by, then eventually a year, all the while your inner critic telling you still owe money. This is where avoiding the subject does *not* avoid you. Now say you owe money to multiple people, or you have many tasks unfinished; a cluttered mind is full of these "unfinished" projects or unorganized ideas.

If you don't learn how to declutter your mind, you will eventually end up with mental anguish and a world of negativity because you cannot escape the clutter triggers. When you notice that you are avoiding or perfecting something, figure out why. When you notice your inner critic is becoming louder, fight the urge to avoid it and listen to it. Slowly declutter your mind by accomplishing the critical tasks you need to do.

Why Do We Think So Negative?[5]

Many mental disorders, such as anxiety, depression, PTSD, and bipolar stem from a broad view of a **negative perspective**. Everyone has negative thoughts from time to time. However, when negative thinking patterns control our minds, it can be very debilitating. Negative thinking can cause unnecessary stress, increased heart problems, and overall unhealthy wellbeing. It's hard to define what negative thinking is because, for some people, it's a way of

---

[5] Smith, E.-M. (n.d.). *What is Negative Thinking? How It Destroys Your Mental Health.* [online] Available at: https://www.healthyplace.com/self-help/positivity/what-is-negative-thinking-how-it-destroys-your-mental-health

life. Some people overthink, obsess, worry about situations completely out of their control, and fear failure. Some take on too much to handle because of their inner empathetic nature. Being trapped in a cycle where negative thoughts and emotions are on constant repeat is when thinking can become an issue. So, what causes someone to endure such negative thinking patterns?

Fear of What Could Happen

We can never truly know what lies in store for us, and perhaps that is why so many people fear the future. It's one thing to be afraid of what the future may hold and something else entirely when you let that fear take over. Negative thinkers often **catastrophize**[6] everything, meaning they predict what will happen and know for sure something terrible *could* happen. There

---

[6] McGauran, D. (2015). *12 Negative Thought Patterns that Play Havoc in Life*. [online] Available at: https://www.activebeat.com/your-health/12-negative-thought-patterns-that-play-havoc-in-life/12/

is no sure-fire way to rid yourself of worrying about the future; however, to overcome these fears is to change your perspective. You cannot control everything, but that which you can control is right here at this moment.

Anxiety About the Now

When focusing on the present, it's hard to ignore the inner critic that often causes anxiety and grief. Many people stress over the little things like their current work performance, the quality of their dinner, or their parenting skills. A negative thinker could be entirely in the moment but then think of the worst scenario in every situation. They may think they are doing horrible at their job, which makes them try to improve, even if their performance was already exceptional and doing more would cause them harm in the long run. You could sit in traffic and think, "My children's teachers must think I am terrible for being late to pick up my kids up every day." There is a difference between *going with the flow* and *obsessing* over every moment. Going with the flow is your best option for overcoming these negative thinking patterns when trying to be better with yourself.

Regret for Past Mistakes

As we are all human, there will always be something we think we could have done better. There will always be those moments when we look back on something and regret the decisions we made then. However, unlike those who move on from the past, negative thinkers will obsess about the past so often they will become upset frequently about their histories. Instead of dwelling on the past, learn from it and realize that it takes failure to grow into who you want to be.

The best way to combat negative thinking, whether it be about the future, present, or past, is to understand it to its core. When you can do that, you can then learn how to question your inner critic and learn what triggers your negative thoughts leading to mental clutter.

Eight Unhealthy Negative Thought Patterns[7]

Let's look at this from an outsider perspective. Have you ever been friends or acquaintances with someone who seems to have horrible luck all the time? Or maybe you have come across people who complain about their life and their circumstances but do nothing to change it. Perhaps you have even witnessed someone try to change, but they are still always so down, anxious, and cynical about everything. This is because their thinking patterns have become so much like second-nature that they don't know that they are even negative. Now, let's change the

---

[7] McGauran, D. (2015). *12 Negative Thought Patterns that Play Havoc in Life*. [online] Available at: https://www.activebeat.com/your-health/12-negative-thought-patterns-that-play-havoc-in-life/12/

perspective back to your own view. When you do something often enough for it to become second-nature, you may feel like the victim in most aspects of your life. Again, this is because you have developed the negative thought patterns that have now formed into daily habits that you can't escape from. No one likes to be around people who are negative, so if you find that you don't have many friends, then you may want to look at your attitude and see your patterns.

As a negative thinker, you may feel perfectionistic, drained from overthinking, or be having a hard time focusing. Problem-solving and decision-making become harder because you are constantly worrying about the outcome, not the approach. As a result, you become mentally cluttered and overwhelmed with stress; to cope with your anxiety, you avoid making decisions altogether. Now you are in a downward spiral because other tasks have come to mind and all you can see are problems piling up with no solutions. *Snap out of it!* This is your mind trapping you inside your inner critic, which will take advantage of your vulnerability. The following are some thought patterns that almost all negative thinkers struggle with.

Catastrophizing

I am late for my appointment, and now I will have to pay money because I couldn't get there on time. I can't afford to fork out hundreds of dollars, so maybe I shouldn't go.

Catastrophizing is when you predict what will happen and then obsess over how it could get completely out of control. From the example stated, the scenario could then escalate and make you think about all the *other* bills and debts you have piling up, which would then have you ruminating over things that bring you the fear about your future. From being a few minutes late to an appointment can spiral to not being able to put food on the dinner table for your children, to then losing them to the ministry, and eventually, becoming homeless. This is catastrophizing.

Avoiding or Minimizing

If I don't talk during the meeting, I have no chance of saying something wrong, and then I won't be embarrassed by it. The result of this is that I will avoid potential embarrassment.

This thought pattern is a coping mechanism for negative thinkers to downplay an event so they don't have to face it. They pretend there isn't a problem as if the problem will deal with itself. The example stated stems from a person fearing embarrassment at work, so they avoid the activity that could push them further in their career to avoid the anxiety around the other outcome. They are minimizing their health and ignoring the fact that they have a problem.

I Should Have / Should Not Have

I should have studied or prepared harder; maybe then I would have gotten that raise my coworker received.

I shouldn't have worn those white pants; now I will never get the stain out.

This thinking trap makes a person feel inadequate because they should have or should not have done something. Negative thinkers like to make excuses for why they can't do something rather than why they can, so they may use the should-thinking pattern as a reason they cannot do something. For example: "I should probably help my mother with her dog, but I can't because I should do things around the house instead." The should-thinking trap gives the person their own personal reasoning so they don't have to take responsibility for the things they need to be doing, leading to procrastination techniques and possibly in the long run, depression. The should statement is an excuse to stay stuck in one's perfectionism mind-frame, believing they *should* be smarter, braver, prettier, etc.

Irrational Decision-making

I'm hurt by what my spouse said to me, so I will break up with them as soon as possible.

Irrational decision-making stems from acting on impulse because of how you are feeling. The fact is that when you are emotional, your rational mind takes a backseat, resulting in the intuitive mind taking over. Sometimes the intuitive mind comes in handy, but if you are emotional, blood flow can go to your muscles instead of your brain, causing a *stress response* to kick in (we will learn about stress responses in more detail in the next chapter). With less blood flow to your brain, acting out of impulse because of your emotions feels like the best answer to your current problems. As a result, you end up regretting or feeling ashamed of your impulses later on, which could induce distrust for yourself in solving problems later.

All or Nothing/Black or White

They told me I'm not good enough, so that means I am definitely not good enough.

I failed at my driver's license test, so that means I'm a failure.

Black and white thinking leaves no room for gray areas in between. It's one way, or it's the other— which also leaves no room for mistakes. Also known as **all or nothing thinking**, it puts pressure on yourself to keep you stuck in the "I'm not good enough" mindset. This cognitive thinking trap will not help you out unless you are in a life-or-death crisis where there is no time to think.

A Cruel Inner Critic

I don't have a relationship, so I must be fat and ugly.

I cannot quit drinking, no wonder no one likes me.

The **inner critic** is loud, annoying, mean, and your own personal bully. What do we do with bullies? We acknowledge them but don't engage in their insults. Negative self-talk is a large factor of depression because the person believes they are worthless and incompetent. When you continuously tell yourself negative things about yourself, you put out an unattractive aura and bring others down. As a result, people don't come near you often, which only justifies what you tell yourself regularly, making the negative habit spiral.

Mind Reading

My father told me I needed to get out of the house more. He must think I am a sack of potatoes.

My friend hasn't called me in over seventy-two hours when she usually calls me every day. She must hate me.

The **mind-reading cognitive trap** is a fallacy in which you assume you know what others are thinking about you. You believe that when someone criticizes you, or when something is out of place, it must be your fault. Mind reading is when you have no sure evidence or validation that someone is thinking wrongly about you, yet you assume that you know otherwise. What you may not realize are all the other factors that may have come into play beyond that one interaction—sure, your father may have asked you to get out of the house, but it's because he loves you and wants to see you outside. Maybe your friend hasn't called you because they lost their phone.

Jumping to conclusions

My phone is gone, so someone must have stolen it.

Similar to the mind-reading cognitive trap and catastrophizing, **jumping to conclusions** is a negative thinking pattern that can leave you stuck in a cycle. Just because your phone disappeared does not necessarily mean someone took it; it could mean that you misplaced it or left it somewhere without remembering where you last had it. Jumping to conclusions is one of the first cognitive patterns your brain resorts to when in panic mode as a defense mechanism to the stress response. First, by predicting we know what someone is doing or saying about us; and second, by predicting our future and the outcomes of our decisions. This can cause more anxiety and fear, which clouds our visions of success and opportunities.

Memorize these cognitive distortions because when you know your trigger, you can start overcoming your negative patterns. The next step is to question that inner critic and take better care of your mental wellbeing so you can trust yourself to make the right decisions. Mental clutter thrives on negativity and low self-esteem problems such as having too much to do, among other issues.

Why Must We Use Positive Thinking to Our Advantage?

Positive and negative thinking is based solely on your perspective and how you see things. For example, if the glass is at the halfway stage, do you see it as half full, or half-empty?[8] This question is a perfect way to see whether someone thinks positively or negatively. The truth about the way we think and our perceptions is that when we feel positive, we put good vibes into the universe. When we think negatively, we develop a poor aura around us that isn't attractive. What we put into the world, we get back tenfold by the universe. For example, if we are stuck in traffic and will be late for our doctor's appointment, we can choose to dream up the worst scenarios which may produce a stress response, or we can decide against these thoughts. The stress

---

[8] Cherry, K. (2019). *Understanding the Psychology of Positive Thinking.* [online] Available at: https://www.verywellmind.com/what-is-positive-thinking-2794772

response feeds us anxiety and alters our problem-solving skills, which can cause actual catastrophes to be out of our control. If we choose to think positively, however, we become calmer and make more rational decisions. As a result, the universe repays us with good luck and fortunate opportunities for personal growth. With that said, we can assume that our thoughts drive our behavior, ultimately defining our outcome.

Positive thinking is not just about thinking positive or implementing good thoughts into your mind, nor is it about seeing the world through clear glass and thinking a rose doesn't have its thorns. It's about dealing with life's complications with a positive state of mind, understanding that stressful events will happen, and not allowing these complications to take hold over our minds. You need not avoid everything bad to live a positive, fulfilling life.

Instead, you need to seek every failure as an opportunity and every situation as a possibility for change. Positivity is about turning adverse events toward a positive perspective. An overall positive person will experience a list of benefits, including:[9]

- Life longevity

- Decreased amount of stress

- More downtime

- Lower chance of depression and anxiety

- Better at solving problems and making important decisions

- Are happier and more confident

- Increased physical and mental wellbeing

---

[9] Cherry, K. (2019). *Understanding the Psychology of Positive Thinking.* [online] Available at: https://www.verywellmind.com/what-is-positive-thinking-2794772

Positive thinkers understand that we are all human, so they make room for mistakes and welcome an imperfect self. They don't make their expectations too high, and they don't react impulsively. Positivity leads to confidence, high self-esteem, and self-worth among many other aspects revolving around the personality.

Ultimately, a cluttered mind hides within the details of a negative mindset. As you read through the contents in this book, you will understand that a cluttered mind is not just about how someone thinks (positive or negative), but more about how they decide to live their life based on their thought process. Almost everything can cause the mind to be overwhelmed with mental clutter. If you have been putting off important tasks, or your workspace is messy, or your life is busy with children, families, and a long-lasting relationship, these things can make a significant impact on your mental health. Aside from living an active lifestyle, we live in a world full of technology and toxic people that can exhaust our minds quickly.

Chapter Two: The Link of Stress and Negative Thinking to Mental Clutter

Did you know that your thoughts play a role in how you feel?[10] Negative thinking can lead to negative feelings that ultimately lead to negative experiences. Often, our thoughts and emotions affect our behavior. Have you ever wondered why you flirted with your friend's spouse or why you didn't speak up when you wanted to? That's because there is a deeper connection between these aspects of our lives.

Thoughts form in our minds about the experiences we go through, taking in all the information we receive and then labeling it as good or bad. Our minds act as a gateway for this information and then, based on how we think about it, our brain determines whether the information we take in is relevant. These thoughts that form around our experiences

---

[10] Nicholas, R. (2017). *How Do My Thoughts Impact My Life?* [online] Available at https://www.chariscounselingcenter.com/blog/how-do-my-thoughts-impact-my-life/

become beliefs that affect how we feel about particular situations.

Feelings are the response we get after thinking about something. The best way to explain this is by taking a simple idea such as "I am hungry" and thinking about where that thought came from. People can be hungry because of an exhausting day or simply because they haven't had a meal in a while. Being hungry can arise from being angry, emotional, or having a busy day. So, the way we feel about being hungry could cause anger, sadness, or contentment depending on the reason the thought came to mind in the first place.

Behaviors come from a combination of these thoughts and feelings. The reason we may act on impulse is that we let our emotions take over. The thoughts that persuade our choices base why we work on our logical reasoning. So, when you have an idea about being hungry, you have a feeling tied to that thought. As a course of action, we then go to the store or in our cupboards and make food. If we are sad and upset, we may reach for comfort food such as unprocessed sugar. If we are angry, we might want something greasy. However, contentment leaves us with many options.

Based on that simple "I'm hungry" example, your thoughts can affect your feelings, and then your behaviors would take place to solve the problem. The problem with negative thinking is that they usually leave us feeling down and upset with ourselves or our surroundings, which almost always blocks our logical reasoning. From that, we make impulsive actions as a method to fix the issue. When we act on impulse stemming from our emotions, we not only hurt ourselves but also the people we care about. Sometimes the result is that they leave us alone, which only justifies the negative thoughts we tell ourselves. If you find yourself in this position, start taking a mental note of your thoughts before defining how you feel and what action you will gain from that experience—you may find that your thoughts are the root of most of your problems. As you read through this book, you will learn new information about how thoughts can clutter your mind and ways to overcome negativity in your life.

Our minds are incredibly powerful, especially when we fuel it with positivity and skills towards personal growth. It has also been said that to keep these learned skills, such as math and language, you need to continue practicing them. Steve Maraboli said, "Once your mindset changes, everything on the outside will change along with it,"[11] meaning that what you feed your mind is what you will receive, and what you give out to the universe will come back to you in your karma. What you think about ultimately defines your outcome, making it your reality. For example, if you think you aren't good enough, you will start to feel it too. As a result, you will slack off on things you aren't good at and not put as much effort into things you *are* good at. These are more justifications for your current thoughts and feelings, making you believe even more that you aren't good enough. It's a vicious cycle.[12]

If this cycle continues, a disorder known as *dissociation* takes place. **Dissociation[13]** is your

---

[11] Oppong, T. (2017). *The Mindset Advantage: How Your Mental Frame Affects Your Behavior and Performance*. [online] Available at: https://medium.com/the-mission/the-mindset-advantage-how-your-mental-frame-affects-your-behavior-and-performance-1b08aa4c2d97

[12] Morin, A. (2016). *This Is How Your Thoughts Become Your Reality*. [online] Available at: https://www.forbes.com/sites/amymorin/2016/06/15/this-is-how-your-thoughts-become-your-reality/#d237edc528a0

[13] WA State CBT+. (n.d.). *What is Dissociation and What to Do About It?* [online] Available at https://depts.washington.edu/hcsats/PDF/TF-%20CBT/pages/7%20Trauma%20Focused%20CBT/Dissociation-Information.pdf

brain's way of telling you that enough is enough and it shuts down, disconnecting you from what is happening and leaving you with **brain fog**. It can happen when you avoid your negative thoughts and put them aside without dealing with them. The chaos stops the anxiety and mental clutter from overwhelming you as a coping mechanism to shut down the stress. While someone has dissociation, they may show symptoms such as

- Mind-wandering or seeming "out of it"
- Blank stares
- Hazy look
- A distorted reality (as if your surroundings are no longer real)
- A lack of control or feeling as though you aren't controlling your movements or thinking.
- Detachment from your identity and your personality

- Feeling out of body
- Overall disconnected

When you avoid your negative thoughts long enough, these symptoms, among many others, may arise; however, dissociation disorder is something that can appear without warning. This means that even though you can avoid your negative thoughts, you cannot run away from dissociation disorder. Some people don't notice these symptoms while others do, which can significantly impact your ability to cope with fear and face trauma. There are ways to deal with dissociation, such as learning **grounding techniques**, so-called because they mostly revolve around the individual snapping back to reality.[14] Some techniques have the individual focusing on a current conversation or making direct eye contact. If no one is present in the

---

[14] Simon, J. (2013). *Kill Stress in Five Minutes or Less*. [online] Available at: https://medium.com/texas-mccombs/kill-stress-in-five-minutes-or-less-1985df4b6f08

moment of a dissociation episode, they can pay attention to how their body touches a surface, like how their feet rest on the ground. The individual can count the tiles on the floor, close their eyes and listen to what's around them, or find ten blue things in the room. Although dissociation disorder is easily manageable, the ultimate way to avoid being diagnosed is to stop avoiding your thoughts. You will learn more about preventing dissociation in chapter four.

What Makes Stress So... *Stressful?*[15]

A cluttered mind can be stressful, and if you combine mental stress with work and life stress, you have triple the burden. Are there ever any moments where you wonder why you struggle with panic attacks, have a depressive episode, or feel out of it for no reason? It may be because of

---

[15] Segal, J., Smith, M., Segal R., & Robinson, L. (2019). *Stress Symptoms, Signs, and Causes*. [online] Available at https://www.helpguide.org/articles/stress/stress-symptoms-signs-and-causes.htm

the stress response that happens when your body and mind are on overdrive. **The stress response** occurs when the hormones cortisol and adrenaline surge through your body, causing it to go haywire. The stress response is your body's way of protecting you when there is a perceived threat, rational or irrational. Another name for the stress response is **the fight-or-flight response,** which is an uncomfortable sensation; however, during a real fight, it could save your life. The release of the chemicals cortisol and adrenaline can help you run faster, hit harder, have quicker reflexes, and stay alert and on guard.

Stress is not all bad as it can help you defeat your weaknesses, rise against all odds, and keep you on your toes. However, if you have too much stress, it can affect all aspects of your life. This can be because our minds are too busy, we have a fast-paced life, or we are listening to our inner critic. When you learn how to relax, you can decrease your stress and live life to its fullest potential. Learning to relax can include breathing in traumatic situations, holding firm boundaries, and dealing with toxic people healthily. **Chronic stress** is a constant feeling of being unable to relax and a belief that you can't escape from the issues in your life. It is when you have too much going on mentally and physically, killing your spirit and leading to chronic stress if not dealt with. Some people are better at handling stressful situations than others, but that is mainly because they have learned how to react in dramatic scenarios. Chronic stress can lead to many health issues, such as:

- Anxiety and panic disorder
- Sleep disturbances
- Depression
- Digestive issues

- Heart disease
- Infertility or pregnancy problems
- Cognitive and memory difficulties
- Unexpected weight loss or weight gain

Many people don't realize how much stress they are under because it becomes a way of life for them. At first, maybe one bill becomes overdue, then maybe you show up late to work too many times, and now you are on probation. From there, you may find that you are always on the go, answering too many phone calls, listening to the demands of your spouse and children, among various other life stressors. This lifestyle can lead to an overwhelming stress load—especially if there is no time for yourself. You may not notice that you are stressed out, but you may start seeing symptoms that can weigh you down even more. Here is a table of many common stress symptoms:[16]

Cognitive Symptoms	Emotional Symptoms
<ul><li>Poor Memory</li><li>Cruel and racing thoughts</li><li>Develop a negative perspective</li><li>Overthinking problems</li><li>Obsessive worrying</li><li>Troubles with concentration</li></ul>	<ul><li>Depression or overwhelming sadness and loneliness</li><li>Anxiety and irritability most of the time</li><li>Constant mood swings</li><li>Self-isolation</li></ul>

[16] Segal, J., Smith, M., Segal R., & Robinson, L. (2019). *Stress Symptoms, Signs, and Causes*. [online] Available at:
https://www.helpguide.org/articles/stress/stress-symptoms-signs-and-causes.htm

Physical Symptoms	**Behavioral Symptoms**
• Undiagnosed aches and pains	• Eating more unhealthy or not at all
• Digestive issues such as constipation or diarrhea	• Always feeling fatigued due to too much or not enough sleep
• Gut instability such as constant gas or bloating	• Using alternative drugs to cope such as cigarettes and alcohol
• Chest pain and increased heart rate	• Unhealthy habits such as nail-biting, pacing, or bouncing
• Decrease in libido	• Withdraw from social activities
• Cold and flu symptoms	• Procrastination

If you have noticed any of these symptoms, it may be because of an overload of or chronic stress in your life. Take a step back and think about how you are living your life so you can assess your situation and fix it. The leading cause of stress is reliant on the individual as everyone deals with theirs differently. For example, one person might feel anxious to get up and speak in front of a large crowd, whereas someone else might flourish in the attention they get during a presentation. On the other hand, that same person who is afraid of groups may have no issues being by themselves, while the other individual may need constant socialization. Some people thrive in the eye of pressure and anxiety, whereas others do not do well under pressure. The causes of chronic stress may include:[17]

---

[17] Segal, J., Smith, M., Segal R., & Robinson, L. (2019). *Stress Symptoms, Signs, and Causes*. [online] Available at: https://www.helpguide.org/articles/stress/stress-symptoms-signs-and-causes.htm

- Life changes
- Relationship issues
- Being a busybody
- Children and family
- Finances
- A cruel inner critic
- Inability to accept change and the unknown
- Black-or-white attitude

So, how can you tell if you have too much stress in your life? The following are some things to consider when facing stress symptoms:[18]

The People in Your Life

If you have a group of people who are supporting and encouraging, such as close family members and interpersonal relationships, you may find that you don't get stressed out as often over things that others do. On the other hand, if you

---

[18] Segal, J., Smith, M., Segal R., & Robinson, L. (2019). *Stress Symptoms, Signs, and Causes*. [online] Available at: https://www.helpguide.org/articles/stress/stress-symptoms-signs-and-causes.htm

have withdrawn from people to cope with the amount of stress in your life, it can lead to an inability to handle more pressure. You must be careful with the company you keep because you may have many people in your life, but some of those people could actually be draining energy from you.[19] This adds to your mental clutter and negativity, which ultimately results in more panic attacks and a higher risk of depression and mental illness.

Ability to Control

They say one thing about control—you are *always* in control. You cannot determine or demand things of others and expect them to listen; however, you can control how *you* act, think, feel, and perceive a situation. When you have complete control or feel that you have

---

[19] Stevenson, A. (2019). *Everyday Habits That Zap Your Energy and Make You Feel Sluggish*. [online] Available at: https://healthprep.com/living-healthy/8-everyday-habits-that-zap-your-energy-and-make-you-feel-sluggish/2/?utm_source=google&utm_campaign=1698316511&utm_medium=search&utm_term=overwhelming%20exhaustion&utm_content=66177941437

control over the aspects of your life, challenges become easier, leading to less stress and anxiety. If you presume that you have no control over your life, and you always listen to the judgments of others, the burden of life and all its stressors will control you.

Confidence and Positivity

Remember, your outlook on life plays a significant role in how much pressure you feel.[20] Developing confidence and seeing things as positive as they can be (given your situation) allows you to manage your stressors better. Negativity and low self-esteem leave you feeling vulnerable and angry, so the ability to "laugh at yourself" in a difficult situation is slim. Laughter is the best medicine to any problem relating to dramatic circumstances, so you must learn to go

---

[20] Cherry, K. (2019). *Understanding the Psychology of Positive Thinking.* [online] Available at: https://www.verywellmind.com/what-is-positive-thinking-2794772

with the flow if you want to become better at controlling your stress.

Emotions

Some people struggle with their feelings and even more so if they are naturally anxious or moody. Others know how to calm themselves through frustration and conflict. The individuals who struggle with soothing themselves in tough situations are the ones who suffer from increased heart rates and racing thoughts. These symptoms lead to chronic stress if the individual cannot learn how to manage their emotional outbursts. Frequently, these individuals do not notice their emotions heighten, so things spiral, which can lead to behavioral issues. It's all about how well aware you are about your feelings that can lead to more resilience and less pressure during the conflict.

There are several more strategies that you can use to decrease your stress, aside from those mentioned above. Exercise is an excellent release for emotional baggage; connection to others can relieve you of sadness; and learning to meditate can ease behaviors accumulated through conflict. You will learn more about these methods in chapter four.

What Actually Happens During the Stress Response?

The three hormones that play a part in releasing the stress response symptoms into your body are **adrenaline, cortisol**, and **norepinephrine**.[21] When a late text from your ex notifies your phone, your heart skips a beat. When you get a call from the hospital, your stomach does a backflip right before you answer—these flutters

---

[21] Klein, S. (2013). *Adrenaline, Cortisol, Norepinephrine: The Three Major Stress Hormones, Explained.* [online] Available at: https://www.huffingtonpost.ca/2013/04/19/adrenaline-cortisol-stress-hormones_n_3112800.html

are your **parasympathetic nervous system** reacting to your experiences, otherwise known as your *fight-or-flight response.*[22] Have you ever wondered what caused the knotted twist in your throat when you hear an unexpected event has happened? What goes on behind the scenes? It's the surge of those three hormones rushing through your body which if not handled through deep breathing or emotional awareness stimulation can cause a full-blown panic attack.

The Limbic System[23]

Inside the brain, you have various parts that take in information such as the hippocampus, amygdala, and the hypothalamus. The **hippocampus** brings in your experiences and turning them into short-term memories. After

---

[22] Klein, S. (2013). *Adrenaline, Cortisol, Norepinephrine: The Three Major Stress Hormones, Explained.* [online] Available at: https://www.huffingtonpost.ca/2013/04/19/adrenaline-cortisol-stress-hormones_n_3112800.html

[23] SoP. (2016). *The Limbic System.* [online] Available at: https://www.thescienceofpsychotherapy.com/the-limbic-system/

your memory has been processed, the hippocampus sends these experiences to the **amygdala** which files the memories to where they need to go. The amygdala then signals the **hypothalamus**, which sends hormones through your body depending how you are feeling about your experiences; for example, *serotonin* is a hormone that is released when something positive happens. Serotonin helps our bodies heal faster and is considered the "feel good" hormone. These three regions of the brain are what we would call **the limbic system**, and it is important to understand the limbic system before learning about stress hormones. If we think we are in danger or threatened, the hypothalamus will release **adrenaline**, **cortisol**, and **norepinephrine**. These three hormones that our hypothalamus releases help our bodies fight off danger, and give us the ability to focus on one thing at a time and make quick decisions on impulse. So, what do these hormones do?

Adrenaline

This hormone is the core of the *fight-or-flight response* system we feel when we think we are in harm's way. The hypothalamus produces adrenaline through the adrenal glands once the amygdala receives a message from the hippocampus saying you are in danger or stressed. Together, the hormones *adrenaline* and *norepinephrine* cause immediate reactions such are heart increase, irregular breathing, and tunnel vision. Adrenaline gives you the ability to run faster, fight harder, and dodge quicker. It also helps you focus your attention on your target, no matter what that would be.

Norepinephrine

Like *adrenaline*, norepinephrine is released from your adrenal glands—but unlike adrenaline, it also gets released from your brain and directly from the hypothalamus region. Because norepinephrine is also released from two places, our stress response is quicker than if only adrenaline were released. Norepinephrine is the arousal hormone responsible for making you feel more awake, focused, and aware. It's also responsible for directing blood flow to essential areas in your body in case of danger, toward your muscles rather than your skin. If there is a perceived threat, it could take about half an hour for the hormones to return to their usual spots after the perceived threat subsides. However, in most cases, it can take up to a few days for the hormones to calm down, which is why it is crucial to understand one's stressors and learn relaxing and coping strategies to combat it.

Cortisol

Cortisol is the primary hormone that is released into our body when we are stressed, known specifically as *the* "stress hormone." Unlike *norepinephrine* and *adrenaline*, cortisol has a bit of a lag and can take a few minutes before being released into our system. The reason for this is that our *amygdala* has to notice that we are in a threatening situation; the amygdala then would take a few minutes to signal the *hypothalamus*. The hypothalamus receives this message then sends the hormone called **corticotropin-releasing hormone** to the pituitary gland, activating the **adrenocorticotropic hormone** which tells the adrenal glands that cortisol needs to be released. Cortisol helps to sustain fluid balance and blood pressure. It also helps regulate unnecessary functions like the reproductive drive, immunity, and digestion, which aren't crucial to your health during a fight-or-flight episode.

Stress relates to a cluttered mind because if you continue to dwell, obsess, and worry about a problem, while second-guessing all your solutions, your body will continue to release cortisol. Elevated levels of cortisol hormones can weaken the immune system, increase blood sugar and pressure, and contribute to weight problems such as obesity. Together, these three hormones are activated to help you survive, which means they work together to give you an instinctive outlook rather than a logical perspective; however, they are not meant to deal with irrational stressors. The faster your response to your cluttered mind, the healthier you will become in the long run.

How to Respond to Your Fight-or-Flight Response

There are a few different methods you can do to lower the risk of having your stress response spiral out of control. It's best to study these techniques so you can stay in the logical state of mind when faced with irrational danger. The following strategies will help you reverse the body's hormones from activating, and if practiced daily, will minimize the number of times they are triggered.[24]

Immediate Stress Relievers

These could include brisk walks, taking a relaxing bath, learning new ways to breathe, taking a mental vacation, and challenging your thoughts. These exercises are quick and you can do them almost anywhere, which is crucial for

---

[24] Scott, E. (2019). *How Your Stress Response is Triggered.* [online] Available at: https://www.verywellmind.com/what-is-a-stress-response-3145148

calming the mind so that the hormones don't take flight.

Refocusing Attention Elsewhere

This technique takes practice and dedication, as it can be challenging to bring your focus from negativity to positivity and enlightenment. Basically, in this scenario, you must change the way you see your circumstances. For example, if you have just been demoted, you can either look at it like you aren't good enough because your efforts go unnoticed, or you can see it as an opportunity to learn from your mistakes.

Build Resilience

You can accomplish this technique over time, though you may not see results immediately— building resilience about your stressors will help you develop a habit around stress relief activities. Over time, stress won't be able to take over and clutter your mind with perceived danger when in reality, you are fine and safe. Resilience activities may include finding your passion, strengthening your positive spirit, making secure connections, being kind to yourself, and growing your decisiveness.

As you bring your focus to yourself, you will understand when you become stressed, what situations bring you pleasure (and which don't), and how you think in certain circumstances. Figuring this out will help you rewire your mind, making the decluttering process of your thoughts and actions a lot easier. Once you learn how to be more resilient with stress and calm yourself in a dangerous scenario, you will figure out where your strengths and weaknesses are so you can build goals and take action sooner. The most valuable part about learning to declutter your mind is that you must keep with it. Make calming your mind and use the techniques in this book your daily routine. Gradually, you will notice a difference when you work at changing your thoughts and turning your life around.[25]

The amount of stress and how you deal with it plays a large part in how much clutter your mind takes on. Clutter is not just about what goes on in your mind—it has an equal amount to do with what happens around you. Your thoughts are in direct relation to your emotions, which ultimately shape your behavior and what you do about your stress. If you don't learn how to manage and cope with your stress, you will only add to the mind clutter and develop more health issues, as explained at the beginning of this chapter.

---

[25] Simon, J. (2013). *Kill Stress in Five Minutes or Less*. [online] Available at: https://medium.com/texas-mccombs/kill-stress-in-five-minutes-or-less-1985df4b6f08

Chapter Three: Mental Clutter Causes — Why Do I Always Feel so Exhausted?

Inevitably, this day and age with digital distractions, earlier maturing teens, and a mindframe to tackle everything forces you to lead a busy life. What many people don't realize is that it need not be just your thoughts and living a busy lifestyle that contributes to mental clutter, but perhaps the primary reason is your surroundings and how minimal you live your life.[26] What's most true about mind clutter is that we can never have two things going on at the same time. So, if you are thinking negatively, and you question your inner critic or challenge

---

[26] Burkeman, O. (2016). *Why You Feel Busy All The Time (When You're Actually Not)*. [online] Available at http://www.bbc.com/future/story/20160909-why-you-feel-busy-all-the-time-when-youre-actually-not

yourself to think positively, your mind can no longer focus on the negativity. For example, when it comes to physical clutter, you can either have your end table in the corner of your living room or your couch—not both. A large box cannot fill up the same space as another large box—it's just not possible. So, why can't we apply these same physics to our minds and our thoughts?

When we multitask, we find that we are actually more behind than we would initially be if we were to focus on one thing at a time. When you dive into the world of personal growth and positivity, it may not work at first even through your best efforts. The number one reason this is is that you have to let go of your negative thoughts completely. You may commit to reading this book, trying out the exercises, starting a gratitude journal, and even telling yourself positive things every day. But, if you have been negative and mentally cluttered for quite a while, you may find that your progress isn't seeming to get you anywhere. Why? Because your negative thoughts also take place. For example, you might say to yourself, "I am confident I will get this promotion today" while still thinking, "What if I don't?" Your mind cannot occupy two spaces at once, so it will automatically choose what's most familiar to it (*the negative*) thus leaving you in the same place you were when you started trying to be positive. So, how do you get out of this for good? More on that, after you learn about how physical clutter can play a role in our mental clutter.[27]

It's the things we see every day but don't notice that take place in our minds. A prime example may be that there are dishes filling up the sink, there are children's toys scattered around the

---

[27] Nazish, N. (2018). *How to Overcome Mental Fatigue, According to an Expert.* [online] Available at https://www.forbes.com/sites/nomanazish/2018/09/25/how-to-overcome-mental-fatigue-according-to-an-expert/#13d19f491644

house, and there is mail just sitting on your end table. The existence of these issues subconsciously reminds you you need to clean them. Now take your busy life—work, making dinner on time, and still finding time for your loved ones, and it's no wonder you are so worn out. Researchers at UCLA have found that physical clutter plays a huge mental impact on our stress, mood, and self-esteem. When our houses look messy, our brains become messy.[28] However, let's say your home is clean and tidy. You may still have a "junk drawer," or clothes that you haven't put away from the summer, and toys you haven't gone through since last year. Many people are taking up a **minimalist lifestyle**, which, as the name implies, is living with less.[29] Although this term may seem like it is easy to do, for most people it's not. This is

---

[28] Mansfield, B. (2018). *The Link Between Clutter and Stress (How to Declutter): Clutter Causes stress.* [online] Available at: https://www.yourmodernfamily.com/clutter-causes-stress/

[29] Brock, F. (2019). *The Single Principle You Need to Clean Out the Mind Clutter for Good.* [online]Available at: https://www.becomingminimalist.com/declutter-your-mind/

because some people believe that our clutter (unimportant things) hold value. They have an attachment to their things, and with downsizing and going through their stuff, they become almost paralyzed because minimizing becomes overwhelming for them. Remember—if you want a decluttered mind, you must dedicate to a decluttered environment. This includes your surroundings and the company you keep. The answer to decluttering your surroundings is to start with one thing at a time. Do not multitask (more on this later); just focus on one room, one closet, one paper, one email, one personality trait, etc.

But how do we develop a clear mind? How can we finally let go of the mental clutter that causes stress and frustration?

1. Mentally move[30]

Metaphorically, our minds are like a vast mansion. This mansion in our minds has rooms for thoughts, worries, desires, fears, passions, goals, questions, beliefs, among other things. Now, tell yourself it is time to *move*. The rent has gone up; the place is falling apart and it's too much for one person to manage. Imagine a smaller place where you will move, such as a cabin with only a few rooms and a few closets. It's time to mentally declutter.

2. Choose wisely what you take with you

As you go through your mansion, you will realize you cannot take everything with you. Ask yourself some critical questions: What am I going to use? How necessary is my inner critic? How often will I use my fears? Am I going to use

---

[30] Brock, F. (2019). *The Single Principle You Need to Clean Out the Mind Clutter for Good.* [online] Available at:
https://www.becomingminimalist.com/declutter-your-mind/

the memories and positive thoughts in this new place? Look at each box inside each room in your mind and decide what you are bringing as if you were actually moving houses.

3. Pick a spot for the new once you do move

Finally, you have officially moved. You have figured out what to bring with you and what you have left behind, and it's time to unpack. Using the rule, *no two things can occupy the same space at the same time*, organize your belongings (*thoughts*) to their designated places. Carefully refile the things you brought with you.

4. Dedicate yourself to this lifestyle

Dedication is about sticking to your guns. There are some items you may have held onto such as your fears and anxieties, but let's hope you also brought desires, passions, and positivity with you. There is a high attachment to our fears and negativity because they are familiar to us. Familiarity is more comfortable to hold on to rather than learning new, and most people find that change scary.

Let's say you brought everything with you to your new little cabin. Your small house is now over-cluttered and your headspace is still confused. But wait—applying the rule from the previous point means that you can store your negativity in a hidden closet or bury it in your yard. By doing that, you can then show off the positivity that you packed and display it on a shelf in your new home.

When you bring the positivity and life goals to the forefront of your mind, your negativity doesn't hold a massive effect on you anymore because you have moved it somewhere else. By doing that, you can then choose the positive thought over the negative one and use it in your reality. You need to focus on this very moment—not tomorrow, not next week, and not even an hour from now. Discard all other thoughts that come into your mind once you focus on the now. For example, if you're going to worry, then pick only *one* worry and obsess about it. Worry until you cannot worry about it anymore, then consciously choose fear and dwell on all your problems right now. When you give your negative thoughts attention deliberately, it won't creep up on you subconsciously and take over living space in your mind. Part of this practice is so that we are learning to focus our attention on stressing about just *one* thing at a time, and so we can keep the negative away from the positive times in our life. You must choose what you will think about (good or bad), stick to that in the moment, then move on. It's so you aren't stuck thinking about both, allowing you to grow out of the familiar and constant negativity.

After a while focusing on single things at a time, positivity will take over your mind because you are still giving attention to your negativity; however, you are no longer allowing yourself to dwell on the negativity, which is good. Once you have completed this process in your mind, you can then say to yourself, "Okay negativity, I have given you attention, now I welcome positivity and I will thrive further than I ever have before." Every day you practice these steps above, you will become one step closer to being free and developing serenity into your life.

The Exhausting Effects of Social Media

A lot of our mental clutter comes from technology and devices, as this is what we use 80% if not 90% of the time. From phones to app watches, from car gadgets to house gadgets, digital technology is all around us. Whether or not we like to admit it, most of us are addicted to technology, specifically social media. The new thing is to know everything about every famous person. We have YouTube channels where you might become well known and famous. We have Facebook pages where we can set up and make traffic for our websites and applications. We have bloggers who use their social media to promote their names. The list goes on, and as it is, most of us already have a hectic life, and social media is part of it.

So why is social media so addictive? How does it have a negative effect on our lives? Why can't we escape it? You may have heard many times that social media and technology is bad for you, but never looked into it. What happens is our brain's reward center lights up when someone likes our stuff. We want everyone to notice us, so when we say something or engage in a social feed that everyone is following and when we see that our comment or status has been *liked*, we feel a sense of accomplishment. Because of this feel-good moment, our addictions become stronger; according to a UCLA study, *social media is more addicting than cigarette smoke and alcohol.*[31] If it's not enough to want to fit in, today's generation of has to know the inside scoop on everything or develop what's known as **FOMO**: the *fear of missing out*. Thirty years ago, if you hadn't watched a movie that everyone was talking about, you would be isolated from your clique. It is a similar situation with social media, specifically in terms of "stories" that we can post on platforms such as Snapchat, Instagram, and Facebook that showcase how we *should* act and look in society. These stories are a major component leading to mental illness and negativity.

---

[31] Cummings, H. (2017). *The Effect of Social Media on the Brain.* Available at: https://www.yourmodernfamily.com/clutter-causes-stress/

What most social media platforms contain are **trolls** or **cyberbullies** who will hide behind social media portraying how their life is so perfect, or how others' lives are not. They tend to be just as lonely as their observers. Whether someone's post goes viral or receives eventual attention, someone else will want to follow this individual, and it comes a competitive game for who has the best smile or life. This affects how people live the longer they dive into the pressure of wanting what the other person has. However, what those pictures and posts don't say is the raw and emotional life that comes with being human. All of this can add to an already cluttered or scattered mentality.

Despite the negatives, we can use social media for growth and positivity. Every human being has the advantage of making their own choices. The information above is mostly about people who have low self-esteem and no control over their personal lives. However, there are some steps we can use to overcome these negative thoughts.

•   **Put down your phone or digital device and take on what is happening around you.**[32] When you practice mindful meditation (more on this in the next chapter), you will develop self-awareness. Being self-aware can help you figure out what you are doing and how it is affecting not just yourself but the people around you. Spend less time in the virtual world and more time learning about yourself and your family members. A rule my grandmother makes every single time we have a family holiday is to leave our phones at the door or turn them off completely. We can check them twice during the

---

[32] Singleton, C. (2019). *Digital Declutter — 15 Ways to Become More Productive and Less Distracted in 2019*. [online] Available at: https://www.stylefactoryproductions.com/blog/declutter-your-digital-life; Cummings, H. (2017). *The Effect of Social Media on the Brain*. [online] Available at: https://www.yourmodernfamily.com/clutter-causes-stress/

holidays, but only then. You may consider incorporating this rule in your own home.

•   **When on social media, limit your time and make it a habit to only follow inspiring and positive feeds**. Ignore reading and commenting on negative statuses and let go of the drama in social media. When you post, make sure they are raw without filters, and in your writings, always try to end your status with a positive swing. Stop obsessing about what everyone else thinks because fortune telling is a stressful clutter that your mind does not need.

•   **Keep note that social media and technology are not real**. Remember that people post what looks like a picture-perfect world because that is what they want you to see rather than what is actually going on in their lives. If most people were who they said they were on social media, consider how many non-genuine and non-creative people we could be in company with. On social media, make sure you are always reading what's behind the scenes and allow yourself to be who you are without being apologetic about it.

When you think about the last twenty or fifty years, technology and social media platforms only started evolving more and more in the past *ten* years. Since it is so new and fresh, there are many more years from now that it will continue to develop. Make a note to teach your kids the safety of the Internet and also make sure they know the social pressure it can have on them. Teach them to be who they are unapologetically by modeling your own confidence. Social media is inevitable; however, just because we are involved in the world of virtual reality does not mean we need to follow everything and succumb to the dark side of it all.

Is Your Life Really All That Busy?

Is your life *really* busy, or does it just feel that way?[33] You may have heard or used the excuse, *there are not enough hours in the day,* to go to work and spend quality time with your family. However, statistics show that the total spent working has not actually increased; we spend more time with our families than in previous

---

[33] Burkeman, O. (2016). *Why You Feel Busy All The Time (When You're Actually Not).* [online] Available at: http://www.bbc.com/future/story/20160909-why-you-feel-busy-all-the-time-when-youre-actually-not

decades. With that said, people who say they are always busy most likely aren't as busy as they think they are. Why is this?

It's because time is more valuable now than it was back then, so if someone can squeeze in a few more hours at work, they will. The pressures of our economy make us have to work harder for our wages than ever before. The fact of the matter is that there will always be something to do in this day and age. We are in what is called **the information era**, which contains technology and smart gadgets that do most of our thinking for us. However, there will always be more emails, more appointments, more phone calls, more research, and more goals to follow through with. No wonder our minds are cluttered—we have so much information to dabble into, which causes us to feel overwhelmed. As human beings, it's our nature to do well and thrive, so in our best efforts to do it all, we don't realize that it is absolutely *impossible* to do everything in a day. This leads us to an indefinite amount of days with endless tasks to do. What's ironic about time management today is that because of the endless jobs that we feel pressured to accomplish, we feel rushed to handle our to-do's. The nature of this era leads us all to feel *busier than we really are*.

The dangers of feeling busy all the time decrease cognitive bandwidth, which takes away from your decision-making skills. Being busy all the time with a cluttered life and a cluttered mind and thinking there is always something to do, makes you more likely to create poor time management choices. If that wasn't hard enough on our minds, we still take on promises we can't fulfill and shift unimportant tasks over top of the necessary tasks, making it difficult to rearrange life schedule. Even the downtime that you have that you want to spend with your family and friends leaves you even busier with no time for yourself. What's the solution?

Slow down—there will always be tomorrow or the next day. By taking on too much and listening to all the demands of others, you train your brain to stop listening to yourself. You need to set boundaries—even with your employers— and take it easy. Look at all the things you do in your day and track it in a journal for two weeks. When you can, take some time to scan through your journal and pick out the things that are of no importance to you. Focus on one thing at a time and realize that life doesn't have to be fast-paced to be successful.

Oliver Burkeman wrote in an article on BBC Radio, "We measure our worth not by the results we achieve, but by how much our time we spend *doing*."[34]

So the question remains—*are you really busy or does it just feel like it?* **Busyness** is a deciding factor among how many activities we have or how long our long list of to-dos is. Some people have deadlines to complete a project, whereas others have projects they believe *must* be done so they can feel satisfied. When there is a whir of activities piling up, we can either feel calm or stressed—and when we have little to do, we can feel scattered. Contrary to opinion, busyness is not defined by how many tasks we have on our list of to-dos; it's just a *state of mind*. Most people try to use the excuse that they are multi-tasking to get things done faster when in actuality we are not; we live only in the moment regardless of our worries. With that being said, is

---

[34] Burkeman, O. (2016). *Why You Feel Busy All The Time When You're Actually Not.* [online] Available at: http://www.bbc.com/future/story/20160909-why-you-feel-busy-all-the-time-when-youre-actually-not

there even such a thing as *being busy*? Or is it merely we feel overwhelmed because we want to be?

Contributing Factors to Habits and Automatic Patterns

Habits are things that we do every day to where they become like second-nature, when you can just do it without having to think about it.[35] Habit and routine can be a leading cause of mental clutter because habits are hard to break. As mentioned earlier, when things become familiar, it develops into habits that are difficult for our minds to break free of. If there is something you have been doing for a long time, you can get used to it without realizing how much mental space it takes from you. For example, if your workspace is always cluttered with both necessary and unnecessary junk, you

---

[35] Gates, D. (n.d.). *Why Old Habits Die Hard!* [online] Available at: https://bodyecology.com/articles/why-old-habits-die-hard/

can then get used to working in this environment. Subconsciously, this clutter is only a visual reminder that you have left things unchecked, such as bills or papers that you have yet to file. The following are more examples of what is contributing to your mental clutter and draining you of your energy.[36]

Breakfast

When you hear the saying that *breakfast is the most important meal of the day*, it's not wrong. However, there has to be a balance with your first meal because eating too much can leave you feeling bloated and slow. On the other hand, skipping the first meal can increase physical and mental health issues later in life. Breakfast needs to be well-balanced with enough protein, grains,

---

[36] Stevenson, A. *Everyday Habits That Zap Your Energy and Make You Feel Sluggish*. [online] Available at: https://healthprep.com/living-healthy/8-everyday-habits-that-zap-your-energy-and-make-you-feel-sluggish/2/?utm_source=google&utm_campaign=1698316511&utm_medium=search&utm_term=overwhelming%20exhaustion&utm_content=66177941437

and healthy fats to keep you going hours longer until your next meal.

Poor Posture

Almost everyone makes this mistake. We want to feel comfortable, and for most people, that means slouching or shrugging while sitting down or standing. However, poor posture can affect our breathing, spinal growth, and lung function. When we slouch or shrug all the time, we are allowing other muscles in our bodies to disfigure for support of the muscles we use daily. Since poor posture often cuts off blood flow, the brain is no longer receiving enough oxygen, leading to feelings of fatigue and exhaustion.

No Spontaneity

We go to sleep, wake up, go to work, come home, make dinner, watch TV, and then go to sleep again. This lifestyle leaves no room for spontaneity and makes for a boring, automatic routine that decreases your level of **dopamine hormones,** which are essential to feeling good about ourselves. You should only have a predictable routine when working; outside of work, we need to learn to dive into our creative sides. Try to do something different every day. When we are stuck on autopilot, our motivation decreases, leading to fatigue and lulls in our energy.

Inconsistent Fluid Intake

Because of the constant whirr of life, it's easy for us to forget to drink water. But as mentioned above, busyness is only a frame of mind in which we use excuses for the time we have or don't have in our day. Researchers have found a direct link between dehydration and decreased energy levels. Try to make it a habit to have water on your person at all times. If having a water bottle isn't enough, set an alarm on your phone or get a water tracking app to keep track of your intake.

Due to these habits or routines, we can be left feeling mentally and emotionally worn down. It's a condition where you would do the same thing over a long period, which sends your brain into overdrive to accomplish the task. Have you felt brain fog recently? Do you feel so overwhelmed or *busy* that you don't feel motivated? Is feeling irritable or moody getting out of control? These are signs of mental exhaustion that result from too much mental clutter. So, what causes mental fatigue?[37]

Decision-Making

What do you want for dinner?

What should you wear to your meeting?

How should you arrange your work schedule?

When are you going to meet a deadline?

---

[37] Nazish, N. (2018). *How to Overcome Mental Fatigue, According to an Expert.* [online] Available at: https://www.forbes.com/sites/nomanazish/2018/09/25/how-to-overcome-mental-fatigue-according-to-an-expert/#1adf0bf16445

Should you hang out with your best friend or stay in tonight?

We ask ourselves questions like these every day, but what's even worse is when other people ask these questions as to put you on the spot. Have you ever had someone ask you to decide for them, giving you a list of things to choose from rather than having them just decide for themselves? Decision-making outs pressure on our minds because secondary questions arise from the original questions. For example, your friend asks you what you plan on buying for your kid's birthday. You have thought about this for months and come up with the deciding factor— you will either wing it or take them shopping. When you give them this answer, they may expect a different result, so they provide a list of ideas. Now you're second-guessing your original thought and are stressed out all over again.

Clutter

As you have learned, clutter relates to stress as it releases extreme levels of cortisol into your body. Clutter is everywhere, but where it should not be is inside your mind. When you have a clear mind, you can picture a clear *decision* on what to do with your life.

Saying "Yes" to Everything

We are human; we aim to please and feel bad when we don't achieve. Making promises or commitments when you already have so much on your plate makes you all work and no play. Overcommitting is another leading factor to stress that is linked to mental clutter because you now have created more pressure on yourself than you originally bargained for. Taking on too much at once may cause a **mental crash**, **burnout syndrome**, and even *dissociation*. This is a habit you need to stay away from.

Lack of Sleep

A healthy mind is accompanied by having up to nine hours of sleep throughout the night. When we don't get enough sleep, we become irritated, unfocused, and moody. These feelings connect to how we behave, ultimately stemming back to how we think.

This may not have been a full list of the causes of mental exhaustion; however, we need to focus more on how to *beat* these habits to stay healthy and on track. The goal is to defeat our inner critics, change our perspectives, and strive towards our future positively. We cannot learn how to master these skills unless we start by changing our habits. So, how do we beat mental fatigue?[38]

---

[38] Nazish, N. (2018). *How to Overcome Mental Fatigue, According to an Expert*. [online] Available at: https://www.forbes.com/sites/nomanazish/2018/09/25/how-to-overcome-mental-fatigue-according-to-an-expert/#1139e98c1644

Be Organized

Staying on top of things can leave your feeling confident and creative because there is no visual clutter that is taking up your mental space. Also, when there is no mental space being distracted by physical clutter, we can focus better on what's important. You can do this by:[39]

- Decluttering your computer
- Organizing and filing your papers
- Cleaning out your emails and unsubscribing to unnecessary things.
- Arranging your bills
- Writing in a calendar for important to-dos
- Keeping a gratitude journal

---

[39] Singleton, C. (2019). *Digital Declutter — 15 Ways to Become More Productive and Less Distracted in 2019*. [online] Available at: https://www.stylefactoryproductions.com/blog/declutter-your-digital-life; Nazish, N. (2018). *How to Overcome Mental Fatigue, According to an Expert*. [online] Available at: https://www.forbes.com/sites/nomanazish/2018/09/25/how-to-overcome-mental-fatigue-according-to-an-expert/#1139e98c1644

Don't Force Yourself to Do Too Much

Perfectionism is another unhealthy habit to partake in. It stems from when we put too much pressure on ourselves to accomplish or get something done in a specific amount of time. It also stems from the idea that others will like us more if we do an admirable job. Ways to combat this are:

- Learn to say no
- Set realistic goals
- Keep tasks simple
- Make time for yourself

Challenge Your Thoughts

When your inner critic gets the best of you, start asking it questions and giving it attention. When you avoid or push away your thoughts to hush the inner voice, you actually create even more mental clutter. Some questions might involve:

- What is the meaning behind this negativity?
- What triggered this thought?
- How can I view this positively?
- Why do I feel this way?

Meditate

A quick way to regain focus is to do a twenty-minute meditation exercise. Meditation can change the way you react to stressful environments or thoughts. You will learn more about meditation in the next chapter.

Allow Yourself to Love Who You Are

Due to social media and the pressure from society, we learn that we must act, think, and feel a certain way to be good enough.[40] Learning to ignore the outside pressures and to love who you are will give you confidence and insight into yourself. Stop trying to impress or conform to

---

[40] Cummings, H. (2017). *The Effect of Social Media on the Brain.* [online] Available at: https://www.yourmodernfamily.com/clutter-causes-stress/

the beliefs and expectations of others and develop a trust for what you believe in. Some ways to practice doing this are:

- Do things you genuinely love to do
- Try something new and get out of your comfort zone
- Start a self-love journal
- Make a positive affirmation list about yourself.
- Look in the mirror and tell yourself one thing you have accomplished in your life
- Set realistic goals and reward yourself for the small things you do.

Defeat Your Self-Sabotage Patterns

Much like challenging your inner critic, finding what triggers your feelings of incompetence is a great way to combat mental clutter. Figure out what you do that disturbs your inner peace and makes you fear change. Some ways you can overcome this are:

- Listen to your inner critic and challenge your thoughts
- Develop self-awareness
- Find your anger triggers
- Ask yourself what you are afraid of when doing something you are unsure of
- Make a decision and stick to it.
- Welcome failure and learn from your mistakes.

To declutter your mind and your surroundings, you should understand what you do automatically through your natural behaviors and set routines. Ultimately, the less stress you have, the clearer your mind will be to focus on other things like productivity and personal growth. Confidence comes from trusting yourself and being fully aware of your thoughts, feelings, and actions.

With decluttering your mind from that which weighs you down, you need to visualize success, then make goals to get there. Similar to the mental move exercise explained at the beginning of this chapter, you cannot get to a place you want to be if you do nothing to change it. When you understand how social media, busyness, and routines affect your life, you can understand how to unravel the patterns that got you here. Having a cluttered mind isn't all about negativity or thinking patterns; it's also about working on every aspect of your life.

Chapter Four: The First Steps to Decreasing the Clutter in Our Minds

Perhaps the most efficient and successful way to fix overthinking habits is to reframe your mind. **Cognitive reframing**, also known as *content reframing* or simply *reframing*, means to look at a situation or scenario and change your perspective or view on it.[41] Often used in guidance counseling or life coaching, reframing is to alter your mindset from a negative or unhealthy thinking pattern to a more relaxed and positive experience. With perspective, the meaning of an experience becomes that of what one views their experiences to be. So, when an individual changes their frame (*reframe*), the meaning behind the perceived experience also changes.

In most cases, when a person changes the meaning behind an experience, that individual's behavior also changes. For example, someone

---

[41] Morin, A. (2019). *How Cognitive Reframing Is Used in Mental Health.* [online] Available at: https://www.verywellmind.com/reframing-defined-2610419

who struggles with a chronic illness may see themselves as incompetent and unhealthy. A more positive perspective of this would be that the illness is a reminder that their health needs to be taken care of throughout their life. Someone without a chronic illness may miss the unhealthy signs, which could cause them to have a shorter lifespan.

When working on reframing one's perspective, questions like "Are there other ways you can look at this scenario?" may be asked.[42] You could also ask if other solutions can solve the problem. For example, when your spouse comes home late after work, instead of jumping to conclusions and getting angry, a shift in perspective would be to ask yourself questions—What is the weather like? If it's raining, your spouse might have been late because of the storm. How often do they

---

[42] McGauran, D. (2019). *7 Ways to Re-Frame Your Thinking*. [online] Available at: https://www.activebeat.com/your-health/women/7-ways-to-re-frame-your-thinking/?streamview=all

come home late? If the answer to this question is never, then what are the chances he was doing anything wrong? What are three possibilities they came back late tonight? In this scenario, the best thing to do is to ask them directly. The difference between *confronting* and *attacking* in relationship situations relies solely on tones, so be self-aware when approaching them with this matter.[43]

Content reframing is an efficient way to change unhealthy habits into positive ones. It can reduce relationship conflict, help you have undisturbed sleep, and give you a significant decrease in anxiety. If you think about it, almost everything we do is content reframing—when we meditate, we train our brains to slow down. When we stay organized and put time aside for ourselves, we are teaching our brain confidence and individuality. When we work on our decision-

---

[43] Craig, H. (2019). *10 Ways to Build Trust in a Relationship*. [online] Available at: https://positivepsychology.com/build-trust/

making skills, we are learning how to focus better and go after what we want in life. This chapter will explain how you can fix the problem by changing the way you live and think about your life.

Why Alone Time is Beneficial[44]

Everything you have learned up to this point helps you understand the dynamics of stress and what a cluttered mind can look like. Your perspective of busyness comes from sacrificing **alone time** crucial to reframing your mind. Being alone with yourself can help you learn more about your genuine self while also allowing you to take care of your priorities above others. Part of why most people sacrifice their downtime is they believe that they always need to be productive. This could not be further from the

---

[44] Kenison, K. (2000). *Why You Must Have Time Alone*. [online] Available at: http://www.oprah.com/spirit/why-you-must-have-solitude-and-time-for-yourself/all

truth because it takes lots of strength to want to sit down and learn more about yourself so you can determine the best ways to be productive. When we don't know who we are and what our goals are, we live our lives on autopilot, doing the same things every day but getting no further than we were before. The cold, hard truth about staying busy all the time is that when we sit with ourselves, our inner critics take flight and we learn things about ourselves that we were afraid of. Have you ever sat with yourself and reached for the phone, turned the TV on, or started cleaning to loud music? The reason we do this is that, for some people, silence is louder than the noise we turn on around us.

Time spent alone can be one of the most exhilarating experiences for figuring out your passions, goals, desires, dreams, and individual growth. When we focus too much on outside stimulation, we often forget about ourselves and don't realize what's important to us. The reason people are set on autopilot is that they get used to doing things a certain way, which programs their brain to think the life they lead is healthy. However, *"normal"* has a different definition for each individual, and even though we think we know what we want, we struggle to accomplish it because of the familiarity we have endured throughout the years. Being alone is beneficial to ourselves for many reasons, those being:

- We become more creative
- It's a cure for what holds you back
- You can see more clearly
- You can gain individual perspective
- You can become your own leader

In the outside world, where we join with hundreds of people and entertainment, we can often forget our reflections or beliefs and adopt the behaviors and feelings of others. Personal growth is about learning to reflect on your own experiences and then fixing the troubles that hold you back. By never allowing yourself to be alone with your thoughts, you can never truly understand your deepest fears, weaknesses, or even what strengths may be hidden within you. If you fear being alone, you must figure out why that may be and use meditation or counseling services to work through it. Part of reframing your mind is about learning to look at something and have a different thought or feeling about it. For example, if you fear being alone because you are scared of not having people around to support you, then you need to focus on *why* you constantly need that support. When do you need that support? Is there a specific situation that requires people for you to be comfortable?

More than that, reframing your mind about that fear is to allow yourself to understand the things that scare you; however, these fears are our defense mechanism to fight off danger. Even if there is no real danger around, while you are alone, you can identify the root of your fear through the experience. Instead of saying, "I am scared of being by myself," say, "Being alone is my opportunity to figure myself out." Reframing your perspective is all it takes to work toward decluttering your mind.[45]

But how do you find time to yourself when there is so much going on in your life? You can start by setting a date and looking forward to that date. Prepare yourself for that moment to come and tell yourself *you deserve attention.* Who better to give you attention than you, as only *you* know how you like to be treated. Make a date with yourself regularly and commit to it. Being alone does not have to be closed behind your bedroom door, reading a book, or meditating by yourself;

---

[45] Morin, A. (2019). *How Cognitive Reframing is Used in Mental Health.* [online] Available at: https://www.verywellmind.com/reframing-defined-2610419

it can be that going out on the town, to a museum, to lunch, to the library, or a walk in nature. Taking time to yourself to reflect on your thoughts is what it means to be alone. The one rule to follow is that you must be *firm* with your intentions. Understand that having someone with you is *not* alone, as this now becomes a group. Instead of walking a path with a friend or acquaintance, have a conversation then politely tell them you are taking time to yourself today and carry on. Good friends will understand and move along too—they too should have some time alone occasionally.

Along the same lines, the next step in finding alone time is to ask for it or gain support from others in letting them know that you will be taking time for yourself on the specific days and times you have chosen. For example, if you are in a committed relationship, you can tell your spouse, "I am taking time for myself this Sunday from seven in the evening until nine. Would you mind keeping an ear out for the children on that day?" Encourage your spouse to do the same for themselves. Their time might involve a guys' night watching football or a girls' day at the spa (or the other way around—girls' night watching football and a guys' day at the spa if they would prefer). Leading up to these times by yourself, you can practice doing absolutely *nothing*. The intention should be that you are relaxing or taking a mental break from your hectic life.

How Staying Organized Decreases Mental Clutter[46]

As mentioned before, one of the main reasons for a cluttered mind is not just about being "too busy," but about being *disorganized*. On average, a person will experience approximately 70,000

---

[46] Bradberry, T. (2015). *5 Ways to Organize Your Mind For Maximum Productivity*. [online] Available at: https://www.weforum.org/agenda/2015/11/5-ways-to-organize-your-mind-for-maximum-productivity/

thoughts per day, consciously and subconsciously. If we ignore our thoughts, we promote overthinking and become a prisoner of our inner critic. When your mind is disorganized, your life becomes cluttered, which decreases your ability to concentrate, letting procrastination take place. One thing to note is that thoughts are *not* facts. A study done by the National Institute on Aging found that a disorganized mind (*mental clutter*) can lead to excessive levels of stress, overwhelming negativity, and impulsivity. Upon these problems, someone may experience real health issues such as heart disease, breathing problems, restlessness, weight loss and gain, and sleep disturbances.

It is crucial to understand why having an organized mind is beneficial. Organization creates creativity and flow, which allows you to be fully engaged in the task at hand with no other distractions. The following are some strategies to stay focused and organized.

Find the Perfect Amount of Difficulty in Your Tasks

If you are bored, you may find that you also become easily distracted by your thoughts because they wander. Daily practice of mindfulness meditation is the best solution to a scattered mind. If something is too difficult, you may lose focus because you are trying too hard at something and getting nowhere in your efforts. Find a balance between boredom and difficulty, and you will stay more focused and organized on the task at hand.

Control Your Feelings

Many people act on their emotions, or in other words, act on impulse. This is mainly because they are not honest with themselves about why they feel how they can do. When you learn to be honest with yourself about the way you feel about a particular scenario, object, or task, it will be easier to react and behave in an organized or collective fashion. Anxiety stems from not knowing how we feel or why, so practice labeling your emotions as they come so they don't seem mysterious, and anxiety will not revolve around your feelings.

Maintain Focus

Studies have shown that it takes roughly five to twenty minutes to become fully engaged in what you are doing. To sustain attention and concentration for better flow, you must persist in your activity for that amount of time. The easiest way to accomplish this is to put away all your distractions, including your phone, the TV, and unnecessary notifications. After the twenty-minute mark of complete focus, you may find the flow you have needed to stay focused.

Breaks Are Necessary

When we do something for too long, we burn out subconsciously. For example, if you are a writer and you get into your flow without taking a break, you may notice your eyes get heavy and your fingers cramp up after working for three hours straight. Although you have been going strong for quite a while, without breaks, your sentence structure may come out disoriented. You may even notice that your ideas go off track. Researchers believe that productive work comes from working for just shy of an hour while having about twenty minutes for a break every hour is most efficient. Sometimes this is not realistic, but try to aim for a breather when you can.

Be Easily Adjustable

The thing about taking breaks is that if you take *too long* of a break, your ideas or focus may not be what it was when you were "in the zone." However, take *too short* of a break, and you may find yourself too tired to focus on what you need to do. Organizing the time your break takes can rest your mind and allow you to continue your task.

Organization is all about *balance*. As you become familiar with the methods above, you will find what works best for you. You will learn what is too challenging for you and what is too easy. You will notice the usefulness of breaks and their length, and you may even start developing a habit entirely different from this guideline. Staying organized means staying on top of things that are most important to you. These five strategies can give direction for the things you do in your life. You can apply it to parenting, relationships, cooking, meditating, and anything else, allowing yourself to be most productive in anything you do.

Meditation is the Only Answer[47]

There is an *endless* list of meditation techniques out there that you can use. This is because meditation is a tool for retraining or reprograming one's mind. It's used in therapy sessions, fitness and yoga, and personal growth. We won't look into all these techniques; instead, it's best to learn the basics of specific techniques for now. Once you have the breathing method down, you can move onto the more profound techniques of meditation, including *self-recognition* and *spiritual enlightenment*. All meditation practices are about emptying the mind and focusing on your breathing. For beginners, it can be tricky to quiet one's mind and concentrate only on breathing. Therefore, you should start with *concentration meditation*.

---

[47] Inner IDEA. (n.d.). *Meditation 101: Techniques, Benefits, and a Beginner's How-To*. [online] Available at: https://www.gaiam.com/blogs/discover/meditation-101-techniques-benefits-and-a-beginner-s-how-to

The purpose of **concentration meditation** is to train your brain to regain focus faster. It helps you practice focusing your attention on one thing at a time, which could be your breath, a word or phrase, one thing in the room, or the ticking of a clock. To start meditation, you could meditate for five to ten minutes until you become more comfortable and experienced, working up to an hour or more. Every time you notice your mind or thoughts wandering, bring your attention back to what you initially focused on. As you get more experienced with this meditation, your ability to concentrate will improve and become more precise.

The next meditation technique almost all beginners will start with is mindfulness. **Mindfulness meditation** allows individuals to watch their thoughts without judging or labeling these thoughts. The purpose is to disconnect emotionally yourself from your ideas so you can find the root of your negative thinking patterns and where they came from. As you become more experienced in mindfulness, there are other mindfulness techniques you can use in your waking life as you are fully conscious. This is necessary to help you become more aware of yourself, your surroundings, and those around you. For example, one way to practice the mindfulness technique is to hold a cup of warm or cold coffee (any drink of choice) and just *notice* it. Look at it as if you were looking at it for the first time. Feel the warmth (or coldness) in your hands and embrace the smell or texture of your drink on your tongue. Make yourself one with the glass, existing together in the same space without being judgmental of each other's existence.

Once these two basic meditation techniques become familiar, you can start figuring out what other methods are comfortable for you. Many meditation techniques include *gratitude* and *forgiveness for empathy.* **Reiki healing** is primarily drawing energy from yourself to heal what's in front of you or at a distance. **Spiritual enlightenment** involves visualization of yourself as being distant from you, your house, your city, your continent, your world, and your universe; the goal is to understand that the problems you face right now are small opposed to what is beyond our attention. Along with these various methods of meditation, each comes with its own benefits. Most of these general meditation benefits would include:

- Decreased blood pressure results
- Reduced overall heart rate
- Less anxiety and depression
- Lower cortisol hormone levels
- Feeling rested, relaxed, and more at peace
- better able to handle stress
- Better sleep patterns

Be careful when you meditate because the *intent* behind your meditation is *everything.* If you expect results right away, you will be waiting forever to notice any difference. However, if you intend to try it out and make it a daily habit, you will see more and more benefits after some time has passed. No matter what your intent is or which meditation exercise you practice, almost all meditation methods follow this pattern:

Step One: Get comfortable either lying down or sitting up.

Step Two: Close your eyes.

Step Three: Continue to breathe naturally, noticing where your breath is coming from—nose, chest, stomach, etc.

Step Four: Once you are entirely relaxed or feel calmer, bring your attention to the flow of your breath. Watch how your body moves with each inhalation and exhalation. Focus on what your breath feels like. Is it hot or cold? Can you feel it in your throat or through your nose?

Step Five: Continue this process, intentionally focusing on just your breathing. When your mind starts to wander, notice it and bring your focus back to your breathing.

In the beginning, your mind may inevitably wander, and that is okay. Part of learning to meditate is that there is no right or wrong way to do it. Each session should last about twenty minutes or more, but for someone who is just starting out, they may only feel comfortable meditating for three to five minutes. Make meditation a daily habit so you can grow towards success and be one with yourself as an individual.

When it comes down to fixing problems in your life, you must realize that beating that inner critic, controlling your overthinking habits, and developing healthy habits requires lots of effort. Nothing worth fighting for is secure, and nothing easy is worth your time. In the following chapter, you will learn more about how to declutter your mind for good and maintain positivity all while looking after yourself. Self-growth is about committing changing your perspective in the way you view negativity.

Chapter Five:
How to Declutter
the Cluttered Mind

Positivity is vital if you want to declutter your mind.[48] With a positive attitude and the firm decision to switch from negative to positive, you develop a sense of peace and happiness. As mentioned before, what you put into the universe, the universe will give back to you, so when you rewire your brain to stick to the positive, you will notice more of the positive things around you, causing your stress level to decrease. What's difficult about being positive is that once you have been in the negative mindset for so long, you become prone to negativity.

---

[48] Cherry, K. (2019). *Understanding the Psychology of Positive Thinking.* [online] Available at: https://www.verywellmind.com/what-is-positive-thinking-2794772

Negativity ends up taking your primary focus unless you can dedicate yourself to challenging your inner critic and choosing to see your life in a different light. The reason it is so easy to be harmful is that in our early caveman years when we were hunter-gatherers, it was instinctive to be on guard and protect ourselves from harm. In those days, the danger was everywhere. Thanks to **neuroplasticity**, *content reframing*, and **cognitive behavioral therapy** (**CBT**), among other practices, we can learn how to reverse this inherent nature within ourselves.

Robert Stickgold, a professor of psychiatry at Harvard University, conducted an experiment revolving around the game Tetris, calling it **the Tetris Learning Effect**.[49] It started when Stickgold went hiking on vacation; when he fell asleep that night, he dreamed of hiking. His

---

[49] Chen, W. (2016). *How to Rewire Your Brain for Positivity and Happiness.* [online] Available at: https://buffer.com/resources/how-to-rewire-your-brains-for-positivity-and-happiness

philosophy was that, in terms of Tetris, the more we play the game, the more we practice it in our waking lives, which can include rearranging cupboards at home, packing boxes into storage, or arranging food on a dinner plate. Stickgold formed a group of college students who played Tetris to play the game in his lab, and then they would spend the night there. The results he found of his study was that over 60% of the participants reported dreaming of Tetris with the pieces falling and being placed together. In a different study from 2009, researchers found that playing Tetris can make the gray matter in one's brain thicker. The Tetris Learning Effect deduced that the more the participants played the game, the easier it became, and individuals would not have to try or think as hard not to lose.

The 2009 study showed how Tetris had the ability to affect the brain's **plasticity** and its willingness to change. The brain makes connections through synapses and by learning something new, and these synapses go off resulting in the connections being more durable and efficient. In conclusion to what Stickgold was looking for, the Tetris Effect Project stated that when you do specific tasks repetitively, your brain becomes used to it—the more you promote optimism into your life, the easier it will grow until it feels like second-nature. Negativity would be a thing of the past, and all you would have to do is change your mindset and the way you worry and overthink things.

Reframe the Way You Think to Promote an Optimistic Lifestyle[50]

With all the information that you have learned about so far, it's easy to understand that by being able to reframe your perspective, you will also

---

[50] McGauran, D. (2019). *7 Ways to Re-Frame Your Thinking.* [online] Available at: https://www.activebeat.com/your-health/women/7-ways-to-re-frame-your-thinking/?streamview=all

influence your thoughts, feelings, and behaviors along with it. For example, someone prone to thinking negatively can see an "off-day" or setback as the end of the world, whereas someone who sees an optimistic perspective will see their down days and let-downs as an opportunity to do better by coming up with creative solutions. So, if you are prone to negativity and pessimistic views, you might wonder how you can change your perspective. The first thing to note is that you need *dedication*, *motivation*, and *persistence*. Just like the Tetris Effect suggests, the more you do something, the more flexible your brain becomes, allowing it to do tasks automatically. The following are a few things you can try.

Watch or Listen to Your Inner Critic

Frequently, we don't realize when we have negative thoughts until we are in a bad mood for no apparent reason. We may try to be optimistic, but it appears no matter what we do, we always have these negative experiences. This is because we are so unaware of our negativity that when it affects our lives, it's become a habit. Other times people may notice their pessimistic thoughts but ignore them, believing they will go away—*wrong*. To start, you must pay attention to when you are feeling *off* and tune into these thoughts. Maybe you had a thought for a split second and it went away, but that very thought could affect your entire day. When we learn to acknowledge our feelings, we can start paying attention to them, noticing the effect that these thoughts have on us. To master this, practicing mindfulness and self-awareness will allow us to watch our thoughts without judgment to get us to the next step: decluttering our minds.

Take Baby Steps

Some people feel overwhelmed with their thoughts and find this to be the reason they push it away. Overthinking leads to excessive worrying, which then leads to a downward spiral of pessimistic views. However, when changing your perspective and trying to live a healthier life, take baby steps. When you think as a child does, you can imagine how their world hasn't been introduced to negativity yet, so they thrive on instinct and constant learning. Babies learn how to sit up on their own, roll over, crawl, and eventually walk and talk. This is the same approach you must use in your own life to turn your perspective around, which can take a lot more work than most people think. Instead of failing and thinking, "I will never be good enough, what's wrong with me? Why can't I do it?" try thinking, "I may have failed today, but it's only a step towards success. What can I take away from this experience? What have I learned?" Similar to listening to your inner critic, notice your thoughts and change them. Do this, again and again, while being persistent and patient with yourself. Eventually, just like the Tetris Effect, you will start to understand it.

Systemic Framing

Systemic framing is a way to think about things from a more significant point of view. Every action results in a reaction, like a domino effect. When you think systematically, you are consciously trying to make sense of your thoughts through observation and awareness. If you did something based on your low feeling, what would happen? Systemic framing is the cause-and-effect way of viewing your environment and behaviors.

Ecology Framing

This thinking involves weighing the pros and cons of your choices. What will happen in the long-run from this decision? If I continue to think this way, what will happen three to five years from now? Is this conflict or problem I am dealing with going to have a lasting effect on my future? **Ecology framing** is about looking at your thoughts, feelings, and behaviors and thinking about them carefully before doing anything. For example, if you were to buy a costly gift for yourself or someone else, how would it affect your relationship or your finances? Can you do it now, or should you wait until you have more money or the gift idea goes on sale? Should you do it at all?

See Failures Differently

This way of thinking is the key to building success. When you can see the mistakes you have made and turn them into growth, you teach yourself how to take responsibility for your thoughts and actions, promoting better decision-making skills. Problem solvers are the ones who can see problems as opportunities. A few things to ask yourself to develop this mindset without overthinking it:[51] What happens if I do nothing? What have I not tried compared to what I already have? Why is this a problem, and why is it bugging me so much? By asking yourself these crucial questions, you allow your brain to think about *solutions* rather than dwelling on the actual problem, thus leading to individual growth and a positive perspective.

These five thought reframing attitudes can promote optimism and create a different outcome than if you were to overthink and continue your negative habits. Each of these reframing methods will help you eliminate failures and setbacks because you are making a change in doing things impulsively. Success in decluttering your mind is about changing your perspective, taking proper care of yourself, and cutting out the unnecessary stressors in your life.

---

[51] Oppong, T. (2017). *The Mindset Advantage: How Your Mental Frame Affects Your Behavior and Performance*. [online] Available at: https://medium.com/the-mission/the-mindset-advantage-how-your-mental-frame-affects-your-behavior-and-performance-1b08aa4c2d97

Now that we have touched on how to reframe your thinking for the better, it's time to learn how to make positivity a habit. As mentioned earlier, a pattern is when you do something regularly that it becomes like second nature. You won't be able to do all the following examples[52] every day, but the more optimism you welcome into your life, the better off you will be and the closer you will be to having a relaxed and peaceful life.

Welcome Positive Influences in Your Life

Let's say you are trying your best to change your mindset and declutter your mind, but there is that one person who keeps bringing you down.[53] Maybe it's a few people. Perhaps it's the fact that

---

[52] Morin, A. (2019). *10 Simple Ways to Always Think Positive Thoughts.* [online] Available at: https://www.lifehack.org/articles/communication/10-tips-make-positive-thinking-easy.html

[53] Stevenson, A. (2019). *Everyday Habits That Zap Your Energy and Make You Feel Sluggish.* [online] Available at: https://healthprep.com/living-healthy/8-everyday-habits-that-zap-your-energy-and-make-you-feel-sluggish/2/?utm_source=google&utm_campaign=1698316511&utm_medium=search&utm_term=overwhelming%20exhaustion&utm_content=66177941437

you are surrounded by the negativity that you don't notice the effect they have on you. We will talk more about toxic relationships in the next chapter, but being around negative people can stunt your personal growth dramatically. Have you ever spoken to someone and afterward felt good about your conversation and even about yourself? This is the *positive influence* you should look to find more of.

Be Responsible for Your Actions

Many people feel victimized by their negativity and search for pity or empathy from others, and will often create excuses to justify their behavior. Often, the individual doesn't realize that they are doing this and the effect of it on other people, but justifying these actions with an excuse can be self-sabotaging. In doing so, you give yourself a reason to continue these pessimistic habits. Instead, understand why the event happened— could it have been because of you? Was it something you said, did, or thought? Take responsibility for the things you have done and make efforts to change the outcome if it were to happen again.

Read Positive Affirmations That You Can Relate To

Not every positive statement is something you can relate to. So when trying to change your perspective and develop positive habits, find phrases and quotes that hit home for you. Find words and affirmations that you would want someone to tell you or that you want to accomplish. For example, if fear holds you back, find a declaration that says something like fear can either keep you back or push you forward—the choice is yours. For anything that you struggle with accompanied by negative thoughts, find an *opposite* quote and hang the words on your wall or write them down on portable flashcards to keep with you.

Replace Negative Wording or Phrases

I can't say this enough, but to get out of your negative point of view, you *must* learn how to challenge every thought your inner critic tells you. Part of the process means understanding the thought that arises, then replacing one word in the inner critic's sentence to something optimistic. For example, take the phrase, "I will never learn from my mistakes. I always keep making the same ones." Instead, you could say, "I feel like I am always failing, but I am always learning." The goal is not just to turn your thoughts into an expertly positive view but to make your perspective more realistic. Absolute words such as *always* and *never* can put so much pressure on you to succeed that your goals become unrealistic—remember the baby steps.

Develop an Ambitious Mindset

A confident individual who has their life and mind together is someone who is goal-oriented and chases after their dreams. It's easy to lose track and fall behind when you have no motive about where your life is headed. Goals and dreams give you the motivation to achieve something greater than yourself. They also give your life purpose, which is the foundation of a decluttered mind. When you accomplish something towards your bigger goals, reward yourself. Or, if you want to inspire yourself gradually, try putting aside 10-20% of every check you receive towards a pleasure buy you can get later.

Compliment and Help Others[54]

It is said that by helping the community through charity work or volunteering, you will gain a sense of profound accomplishment, as this behavior increases the *serotonin* and *oxytocin* levels in your brain (which are the "feel-good" hormones). The same goes for when you compliment people. A spark goes off in our minds releasing these feel-good hormones, and it also allows us to feel empathy and assurance by being able to make someone else's day. To add, by handing out affirmations to others, you give positive vibes into the universe and can likely receive the same if not better treatment later on. When you praise someone, make sure your compliment is genuine and honest; otherwise, your best bet is to say nothing at all.

---

[54] Chen, W. (2016). *How to Rewire Your Brain for Positivity and Happiness.* [online] Available at: https://buffer.com/resources/how-to-rewire-your-brains-for-positivity-and-happiness; Morin, A. (2019). *10 Simple Ways to Always Think Positive Thoughts.* [online] Available at: https://www.lifehack.org/articles/communication/10-tips-make-positive-thinking-easy.html

When you strive to do one to three positive things every day, you may feel lighter and more relaxed on a deeper level.[55] These positive habits are the soul's medicine to being mentally well. Continue to see the positive in every day; congratulate yourself for getting out of bed because others don't have that strength right now. Be thankful for the things you have and the relationships you value now and every day. Define the consequences of negativity and see happiness in all aspects of your life. Make someone smile, or start by just being kind to nature and animals. Eventually, you will develop optimism you won't even notice it until one day when your once-negative thoughts have turned joyful and less stressful.

---

[55] Chen, W. (2016). *How to Rewire Your Brain for Positivity and Happiness.* [online] Available at: https://buffer.com/resources/how-to-rewire-your-brains-for-positivity-and-happiness

Be Your Own Best Friend[56]

Our minds are so busy daily with over 70,000 thoughts reaching our conscious mind on the daily, and that's not even counting the subconscious thoughts. Another way to look at a relaxed and decluttered mind is when you finally feel as though you aren't always thinking. It's when you feel as though there is little to nothing stressing you out, and you are confident in your self-esteem and feeling less pessimistic. Doesn't this sound like something you would want for one of your closest friends?

If *yes* is your answer, then who's saying you can't want that for yourself too? This is what it means to be *your own best friend*. When you learn how to take some time for yourself, challenge your insecurities to new lengths, and be your support

---

[56] Goodlet, N. (n.d.). *5 Ways to Become Your Own Best Friend*. [online] Available at: https://www.lifehack.org/articles/lifestyle/5-ways-become-your-own-best-friend.html

person, you will grow a new sense of independence. This autonomy will leave you feeling better about yourself, ultimately raising your self-esteem. So, what is our definition of a **best friend**? This is generally someone you can rely on, talk and vent to, pick you up when you are down, and be your partner in crime when life hits you hard. Whatever you want in a best friend, try to become yourself for yourself so you can feel better about being an individual. The following are strategies for becoming your own best friend.

Be Kind to Yourself

Whether you develop a positive mindset or if you have become familiar with your negative attributes, everyone beats themselves up. You must make an effort to be kind to who you are, so you can be the best friend you would want for someone else, for yourself. This would include building yourself up when you are down, setting realistic goals, and letting go of your perfectionism. Make a list of all the things you like or have heard about yourself.[57] Are you stronger than you give yourself credit for? Are you creative? Honest and genuine? What are the talents that you are good at? When that cruel inner critic starts to bring you down, ask yourself—why would I ever say this to one of my best friends? This can change your way of thinking almost immediately.

Hold Firm Boundaries to Your Own Needs

We all have needs, but most of us ignore or push aside these needs because we believe that honoring them can be selfish. However, what would you say to a friend who desperately needed self-care and control? You would want the best for them and probably tell them they

---

[57] Dowling, D. (n.d.). *4 Ways to Be Your Own Best Friend.* [online] Available at: https://www.mindbodygreen.com/0-15298/4-ways-to-be-your-own-best-friend.html

need to be selfish sometimes to get where they want to go. The same goes for you.

There is a big difference between being *selfish* and being *self-centered*. **Selfish** is when you work on yourself and try to grow towards personal growth such as quieting your cluttered mind and developing positive habits. **Self-centered** means to think only of yourself and forgetting the needs of others because you feel entitled and above everyone else. There is also **narcissism**—the *me, me, me* factor. Take your advice on what you would say to one of your friends and be more selfish.

Take a Step Back

When we get too involved with our drama or the drama of our spouse and interpersonal relationships, so our thoughts become clouded which disallows us to think clearly. We have an emotional attachment to everything going on around us and inside us. Remember that thoughts and facts are not directly related; thoughts are merely brought on by our reaction to our environment. If you struggle with conscious thoughts about how you are a failure or that you can never be enough to accomplish anything, *take a step back.* This is what mindfulness practice helps you achieve—it's when you can take a step back, emotionally detaching yourself and viewing your thoughts as just words or sentences. By doing this, also take a step back and evaluate your beliefs so you can find a clearer view of how you feel. It will also help you challenge those negative words and replace them as learned earlier.

Be Compassionate and Forgiving of Your Own Pain

Compassion is the ability to accept what is happening in the moment and be at peace with it. It does not involve labeling or criticism. It is not judgmental, nor is it cynical. Being **self-**

compassionate means to let yourself know that things will be alright and giving yourself a warm embrace the same way your mother did. True self-compassion means that you can count on yourself to be there for your pain and acknowledge that it takes time to heal.

Compliment Yourself[58]

When you are unsure of your outfit or your hair, or when you have doubts about how your date will go, tell yourself the things your best friend would say to you. Even if you don't believe it, the chances are you will probably feel better by complimenting yourself, leading to you gain more confidence in your upcoming event. Every morning when you wake up, tell yourself something you like about yourself. If this becomes too difficult, ask a friend of yours to write something truthful they think of you and

---

[58] Dowling, D. (n.d.). *4 Ways to Be Your Own Best Friend.* [online] Available at: https://www.mindbodygreen.com/0-15298/4-ways-to-be-your-own-best-friend.html

put it on your bathroom mirror as a reminder. Once you see this same thing every day, your brain will start to recognize these sayings, and it will happen automatically without effort.

Be Aware of the Things That Distract You

As learned previously, part of mental clutter is the daunting list that sits on your dresser or in the back of your mind of all the things you still have yet to do.[59] Know of these distractions and make it a habit of getting rid of one of the to-dos once a day. Make sure that your *eyesores*—clutter around your environment[60]—get taken care of as well so that these do not distract your mind from developing positive habits.

---

[59] Best, J. (2018). *Mental Clutter*. [online] Available at: https://www.apdo.co.uk/mental-clutter/

[60] Mansfield, B. (2018). *The Link Between Clutter & Stress (How to Declutter)*. [online] Available at: https://www.yourmodernfamily.com/clutter-causes-stress/

Be Tough on Yourself in the Right Way

Do you overeat or under-eat when you are stressed? Do you max out your credit card to make yourself feel better? Do you skip your morning workout some days because you don't feel like it? These habits can slowly turn into bad ones, resulting in expensive debt, weight problems, and laziness. The exercises taught through self-care such as eating right, exercising more often, and taking much-needed downtime are exercises that produce a healthy mind. If these tasks are forgotten, then a pattern of old habits repeating themselves will only make you feel worthless and pessimistic all over again. Do not let these old habits surface and give yourself some tough love to get these things done. Remember the Tetris Effect?[61] Do something enough until it doesn't feel like work, and you

---

[61] Chen, W. (2016). *How to Rewire Your Brain for Positivity and Happiness.* [online] Available at: https://buffer.com/resources/how-to-rewire-your-brains-for-positivity-and-happiness

will gain knowledge and perspective for a healthier life.

Another thing you can do is get inspired and genuinely happy is to write a letter to yourself.[62] Write a letter and pin it up; it should say something like:

I am here for you; I love you and I accept everything about you. I will pick you up when you are down, and I will be there in your best moments. I will help you choose positivity, and I will accept you for all that you are, including your faults.

Take a moment and read this letter back to yourself. What do you feel? Does it feel silly or motivating? Does it feel weird, or does it represent who you are on the inside? No matter

---

[62] Dowling, D. (n.d.). *4 Ways to Be Your Own Best Friend*. [online] Available at: https://www.mindbodygreen.com/0-15298/4-ways-to-be-your-own-best-friend.html

what you think, don't ignore the real feelings that will come of this as learning how to be your best friend takes both strength and guidance. Just as there is no right or wrong way to love someone else and care for them, such is the same for yourself.

Chapter Six: Organizing Your Relationships

Believe it or not, the relationships you keep in your life make up about 80% of what influences you and your thought patterns. For example, if you are always around a cynical friend, you will probably feel the cynicism through their aura, their energy, and their body language. Almost all communication that we use daily is *nonverbal.* So, when we catch vibes and get a knot in the pit of our stomachs, it's our intuition or instinctive nature pointing to something in someone else's demeanor. Another example is if you were interacting with someone confident and comfortable with themselves to where they give off positive vibes. This positive feedback can make you feel good about yourself too, which will depict your thoughts, feelings, and behaviors in the present moment. A cluttered mind is about what you tell yourself along with what and who you surround yourself with. Your thoughts are the foundation of what you let happen in your life.

When you take a step back and look at people who appear to have their lives together, you may observe that they have a job they love, a family they care for, and enough downtime to enjoy themselves. However, if you inspect closer, you might see that their world isn't exactly perfect, but the company they keep is supportive. Life is always moving forward, and many relationships fill the void of loneliness, promoting *self-love*. However, toxic and unhealthy relationships can increase the likelihood of *mental destruction*. All affiliations are demanding, taking both work and your attention, whether these people are friends, foes, family, or life partners. The connections you make in your life are there to support you and lift you up or bring you down and take advantage of you. By looking into the relationships in your life, you can start organizing them and figuring out which ones are the ones to keep around and which ones are best to cut out.

We will first look at what it takes to make healthy relationships; then you can figure out what the toxic ones are in your life. By the end of this chapter, you will clearly understand which relationships can cause you mental clutter, and which will not.

What Makes a Relationship Healthy?

Everyone's definition of a healthy relationship is different, but for argument's sake, let's say a healthy relationship is one that both parties put in work and effort to make a long-lasting connection. Upon first meeting someone, we automatically judge the relationship we have with this person. We determine whether they feel closer to home (*family*) whether they feel of interest (a *romantic partner*) or whether they feel like guidance (a *friend*). As you get to know this person, you think, feel, and act in different ways in your attempts to shape your relationship into what you hope for it to be. For example, if you feel romantically interested in the person, you will turn on your charm and flirt; whereas, if you feel more of a personal-guidance vibe from this person, you will test if you can trust them or not by telling them secrets that wouldn't matter to you if they got out.

In truth, no matter which connections you have in your life, all healthy ones should revolve around a few essential factors first:[63]

Honesty

A primary element to recognize is the amount of *sincerity* portrayed in your relationships. You can be on guard with this one, as toxic relationships can feel honest when in reality, they are based on *manipulation*.[64] While you are reasonable and secure in your budding romance or future business partner, they could have other

---

[63] Neustaeter, B. (2016). *10 Things That Hold More Importance in a Relationship Than Love.* [online] Available at: https://www.narcity.com/ca/on/toronto/dating/10-things-that-are-actually-more-important-in-a-relationship-than-love

[64] *7 Types of Toxic People and How to Spot Them.* (n.d.). [online] Available at: https://www.scienceofpeople.com/toxic-people/

intentions. Being honest on both ends can promote structure and stability in any relationship.

Respect

This one is tricky because often, the way we treat ourselves models behavior for *others* for how to treat *you* too. For example, if you bring yourself down vocally or become too busy to be interested in yourself, your friend, business partner, or partner may treat you the same way over time. As supportive as this person might be in the beginning, it can be a challenging and daunting task to bring someone else up consistently. *Respecting yourself* promotes the respect of others to recognize you and treat you the way you deserve to be treated. For a healthy relationship to develop, there must be mutual respect on both parts to make it last a long time.

Communication

Communication comes in several forms and, more often than not, can be misinterpreted on many levels. If your body language doesn't match what you are saying, or your tone doesn't match your emotional aura, then others can misunderstand you very quickly. Also, in communication, there has to be a follow through with what has been said; otherwise, it can build an area for *distrust*. You may have difficulties understanding each other if you come from different cultures or have been raised differently; however, this is where communication is *key*. Learning how the other person interprets what you say while also learning how to come off better verbally are areas you and your relationships can work together to promote healthiness. Communication is about learning how to listen, while also being able to send the right message.

Happiness

Arguments are unavoidable; however, you need *satisfaction* to develop healthy relationships because it will help make these disagreements easier to cope with and move on from. If you are unhappy and arguing all the time with no resolutions, it will seem like there is no point in carrying on. If you love or care genuinely about the person, you may have conflicted feelings of letting go. This can complicate any scenario because instead of focusing on your relationship, you focus on your internal beliefs, causing happiness to slip further away.

Compromise

Are you mostly a *taker* or a *giver*? As the names imply, **takers** are people who take a lot and give a little, while **givers** are people who give a lot expecting nothing in return. We find givers to be more empathetic and taken advantage of because of their kind nature. However, relationships are about both giving *and* taking, whether you are in a committed marriage or a business partnership. In disagreements, there has to be some middle ground. If your friend, family, or partner asks something of you, figure out the risk of what they are requesting and the consequences if you don't. Do nothing you feel you would end up with an unhappy result. Then, think about the times when they have given something up for you. Compromise is all about decision-making and boundary setting so you don't walk all over them and they don't take you for granted either.

Independence

Contrary to popular belief, spending all your time with someone can *damage* your relationship and your identity. Without independence comes codependency, ultimately taking away from what you most want and what they most want. It's okay to depend on your friend or partner for things, but relying on them for everything creates a dependent habit because it becomes more difficult to think for yourself or do things on your own. When you finally break out of your zone and do something for yourself, your family member or coworker may feel *resentment* towards you because the pattern has formed that you go to them for everything. Independence is one thing you should never give up in any relationship.

Partnership

Also known as equality, a partnership is about how both of you pull your weight in the relationship. You cannot be the only one trying or picking up the slack while they are okay with getting a free ride and vice versa. No person is one's maid, parent, or nurse all the time, and although it's okay to play these roles, it has to come from *both* parties. When you come together and work as a team, you promote a healthy relationship.

One thing left out of this list is **trust**. That's because trust is the main ingredient for all these items on the list. If you don't have faith, then how can you trust someone is telling you the truth when they communicate? Without trust, there is no respect, nor will there be any happiness because that will be the main topic of all your arguments. Trust goes both ways, and once someone breaks the trust, it can be near impossible to get it back. This leads us to our next topic.

Maintaining Trust[65]

Like everything in a healthy relationship, trusting someone goes both ways. Often, we give trust subconsciously and with little thought. For example, when you step onto a plane to go on a vacation, you trust that the pilot will not crash your flight and will ensure your safety. We can

---

[65] Craig, H. (2019). *10 Ways to Build Trust in a Relationship*. [online] Available at: https://positivepsychology.com/build-trust/

also give it when we tell someone a massive secret about ourselves—we trust that secret will be kept in confidence. For those who are more skeptical, they may have a more difficult time believing someone because of their past experiences. So, for those of you who are more skeptical, the question remains—how can you build and maintain a trusting relationship again?

It all starts when you take a moment and think about things from the other party's perspective. They have most likely been hurt too, but are you the friend or foe of the past? You are probably trying to be the friend. With trusting people, you must first build *their* trust and be willing to understand their trust patterns.

Trusting Someone Takes Time

Allow yourself to recognize that things cannot be rushed. Getting to know someone fully takes time, effort, patience, and trust is earned along with respect and honesty. Building trust is about taking small steps; baby commitments can help build communication within your relationships. Over time, you can start accepting more significant responsibilities because there will be a clear foundation for honesty. Remember the give-and-take rule?[66] If you are giving someone else the trust, you will most likely receive some in return.

Think First

Mostly when we are comfortable around someone, we feel the need to open up and trust them with things we wouldn't normally with anyone else. This can sometimes come back and bite us in the butt if we aren't careful, however. To avoid this, continue to understand the person

---

[66] Neustaeter, B. (2016). *10 Things That Hold More Importance in a Relationship Than Love.* [online] Available at:
https://www.narcity.com/ca/on/toronto/dating/10-things-that-are-actually-more-important-in-a-relationship-than-love

better and think before you act too quickly on impulsive feelings.

Be Empathetic Toward Others

Empathy is a trait in which you put yourself in someone's shoes while also having the same strength to disconnect from involving yourself. It is good to feel empathy for someone, but make sure that your own boundaries are in place so they cannot take advantage of you. Role model this behavior too by not taking others for granted and valuing the trustful relationships you have. Understand what it means to give and take, as you can easily break trust when you or someone else feels that there was too much given without the same in return.

Be Honest About Your Feelings

This rule means that you should always be honest while also being aware of how *you* are feeling. Honesty is the best policy when trying to build and maintain trust with someone. However, never hide your feelings either. If you trust someone, then you should always be comfortable being honest with them about the way you feel. If you find that you are having a hard time opening up about your emotions, then this is your intuition telling you you should take a step back and figure out why you can't.

Always Make Sure You Do What's Best for You

This one may seem a little selfish, but it's just like in the example previous section—selfishness is about striving towards personal growth, self-centered is when you make everything about you and no one else. Part of doing what's best for you is trusting your gut and staying firm with your morals and boundaries. If someone tells you something in confidence but something doesn't feel right, lay down some guidelines. Make sure they know you won't tell anybody and they can trust you, but politely discuss that the topic is uncomfortable for you and there is probably someone better to talk with. Honesty and trust go hand in hand. When you stay true and firm to your boundaries, others will see this as encouraging and will even respect you more. Respect comes from people who value your opinion and see you as someone who will stay honest with themselves even when the other party disagrees. It's better to remain loyal and honest than it is to create a lie or not tell the full story.

Take Responsibility for Your Actions

You can attract more positive people in your life by taking credit where credit is due and not blaming other people. If you have ever had a friend who always seems to have an excuse for the things they do, you may feel as though you cannot trust them with certain things. It works the other way around too, so admitting to your mistakes and apologizing without justifying when you are wrong are great steps forward. People grow strong and healthy relationships by feeling like they can relate to one another. If you portray the idea that you can do nothing wrong, then you create a barrier for connection, as the person may feel there is an unnecessary difference between you and them.

These rules apply in every relationship, including those with your friends, family members, bosses, coworkers, strangers, and partnerships. If someone has broken your trust, it can be difficult to trust them again. One thing you need to think about is if they have ever broken your trust before the incident. If it was one mistake, and they are probably genuine in trying to regain your confidence back, and it might be beneficial to go over your relationship. If they have broken your trust on numerous occasions, then it may be a bittersweet goodbye for now. If you are holding on to the betrayal, it could be more of an internal issue in bringing back past hurt and blaming them for it. It's up to you to determine whether you can and want to forgive someone after breaking your trust. This can be tricky because it means you have to build *self-trus*t to forgive and move on from the experience.

Building and maintaining trustful relationships are the foundation for strong alliances. As difficult as it is to trust someone or receive trust from someone, it all starts from trusting *yourself* first. When we believe in ourselves, we can gain more confidence in our decisions and choose whether to let someone go. It also builds our self-esteem in identifying and letting go of toxic and unhealthy relationships.

Identifying Toxicity[67]

Several people are toxic to your health, and you may not even realize it. They can be family members, close friends, or your romantic partner. One of the main reasons you may not notice if you are interacting with a toxic person is because you may not know that they are toxic. It is human nature to stick with what is familiar and most comfortable in our lives[68], and so we ignore the negative things that are happening hoping things will sort themselves out. However, this rarely happens. Instead, we trust that no change is necessary because of the bond we have created. For example, how would we ever suspect our *parents* to be toxic when they are the ones who raised us? We are supposed to trust them and reach to them for guidance and support. How will we ever recognize when our best

---

[67] *7 Types of Toxic People and How to Spot Them.* (n.d.). [online] Available at: https://www.scienceofpeople.com/toxic-people/

[68] Brock, F. (2019). *The Single Principle You Need to Clean Out the Mind Clutter for Good.* [online] Available at https://www.becomingminimalist.com/declutter-your-mind/

interests are not in the heart of our peers? What about our partner who we have gone through so much with? Are they also toxic?

The thing about familiarity and safety is that we create our own version of what is secure in our own minds. Once this is in place, it's hard to see the negative in the people we share our company with. Instead, we make excuses that justify our loved one's actions and continue to try harder in hopes they can change. This way of thinking causes mental clutter and drags you down more than you dragging yourself down. Does this sound familiar to you? You may now wonder who is toxic in your life? How can you declutter these relationships without feeling guilty about it?

There are various kinds of toxic people in the world. The following outlines six of them.

The Narcissist

The classic **narcissist** takes all the oxygen in the room as the most self-centered people on Earth. They lack empathy for others, are entitled, and appear passive-aggressive among other traits. Some would argue that most people on Earth are narcissistic; however, it is not a problem unless they portray it in every aspect of their lives. Narcissists will manipulate people to get what they want and use others' weaknesses to make them feel guilty whilst ever taking responsibility for their actions. With toxicity, narcissists are number one on the list.

The Control Freak

The name speaks for itself. A **control freak** is someone who wants to control everything, make things their way, and views their opinions as perfect. They judge every action you make, every thought you have, and convince you that their way is better. You may hear them complain about things that didn't go their way, so they had to do things themselves. In a relationship, you might find that this person nags you about everything and holds too high expectations of you to control you.

The Emotional Sponge

Whether they be emotional, mental, or physical, it's safe to say that a sponge is a sponge. These toxic people will make you feel emotionally or mentally drained on the daily. They constantly complain about their problems and always see things negatively because they have nothing positive to say. Sometimes it can get better, but often it doesn't unless they take steps to clear their baggage or seek counseling.

The Drama King/Queen

Do you know someone who thrives on drama and attention all the time? With these people, there is always something wrong; when one problem is solved, another replaces it. When you try to give them your opinion or advice, they feel objectified and get angry with you. This is because their sole intention behind coming to you with their problems was to seek sympathy and pity for their circumstances. You could see a clear fix, but with **drama kings/queens**, they will always find every excuse for why they can't or that they already tried it. Drama queens/kings are always in crisis mode because they feel important when they have a busy and dramatic lifestyle.

The J.J.

J.J. stands for a *Jealous-Judgmental person.* Have you ever sat down with someone and it felt like they were secretly judging you during the entire conversation? Their advice is almost contradictory and condescending. Jealousy stems from having super low self-esteem and confidence levels. They have so much internal self-hate that they project their feelings onto you. From this comes judgment in which they feel as though everyone around them is incompetent, uncool, or "out to get them." These people thrive on gossip, making it dangerous to trust them. They never have your best interests at heart as their *J.J. trait* sees nothing above their resentment of you.

The Tank

Sadly, more often than not, you will see *the tank* as someone at the top of the business ladder. **A tank** is someone who goes after what they want and doesn't have a problem crushing anyone who stands in their way. If they believe you will be a barrier in their path, they will bring you down without a second thought. Tanks are arrogant, non-empathetic, and egoistic. They see every conversation, person, and event as a challenge or a game that they must win to receive recognition for their intelligence.

If anyone has popped in your head while reading through this list, it is best to think through much-needed actions so you can take steps to rid them from your trusted circle. That's not to say that you have to cut ties completely, but it may be best to loosen your grasp of them gradually. Understand that by holding onto your attachment of these relationships, you are producing unnecessary mental clutter, which decreases your ability to think. Know what you deserve for yourself a minimize the interaction you have with them while focusing on gaining more positive influences in your life.

Chapter Seven: Maintaining a Peaceful Mind

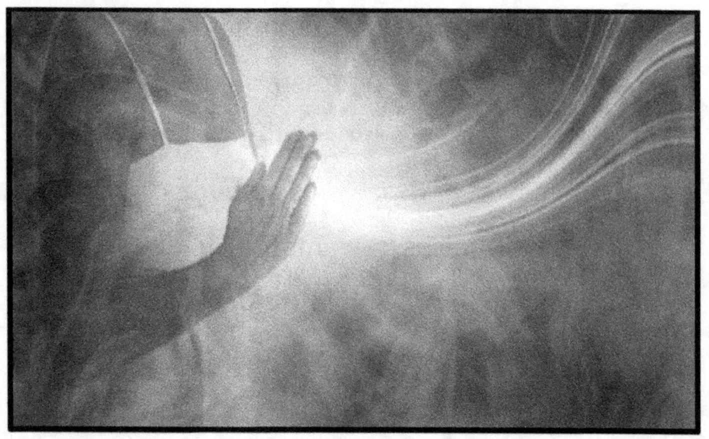

Everything you have learned so far is necessary for decluttering your mind overload. But the main problem that arises when changing our lives is that old habits can creep in and take over. As much as we try to change our thinking patterns, see a different perspective, declutter our physical space, cut down on digital clutter, and seek healthy relationships, our old lives will start breaking through the surface with even one mistake. It's easy to understand why—habits die hard because we are so used to doing them we have automatic patterns for when we fail, and in response, our brains switch back to the old ways.[69] Sometimes we can start thinking negatively and develop toxic relationships gradually until we are sitting with ourselves and thinking, "How did I get here?"

The thing about habits that most people don't realize is that some habits result from *long-term patterns*. For instance, when we were children, we learned so much from our environment, parents, and peers. These surroundings could be healthy, or unhealthy depending on how you

---

[69] Gates, D. (n.d.). *Why Old Habits Die Hard!* [online] Available at: https://bodyecology.com/articles/why-old-habits-die-hard/

were raised. This includes your home and personal life, your role models, your culture and society, and your language. When we are teenagers and young adults striving to make sense of adulthood and the changing universe around us, we take what we have grown up with and carry it on through our lives. Some of these patterns are unhealthy, however, and regardless of how hard we try to change our negativity and toxicity around us, our old habits may come back at any time and damage our futures. You are not completely doomed though, as mentioned in chapter five, the Tetris Effect will work if you take the time to implement the technique in the areas of your life you need it most.[70]

The reason old habits are so hard to break is that they are formed in the area of the brain called the basal ganglia, which remembers pathways

---

[70] Chen, W. (2016). *How to Rewire Your Brain for Positivity and Happiness*. [online] Available at: https://buffer.com/resources/how-to-rewire-your-brains-for-positivity-and-happiness

which nerves and neurons fire on. The basal ganglia is mostly responsible for habit formation, short-term learning process, and addiction. Any new pattern or habit that you try to form or practice can trigger and old one making the brain connect similarities which is why habits and addiction can be quite difficult to break. However, by practicing new routines, and sticking with new habits that you try to change, the same region of the brain makes new connections which makes it easier to stick with the new forming habits. It's best to keep this in mind if you are serious about making a necessary change in your life. It takes approximately ninety days for a habit to be fully implemented into your life, meaning after ninety days of hard work to change the old habit, your new one will run on autopilot.

With that being said, how do we change our habits and make them stick? The first step is to determine which part of your life you want to change; in your case, it would be your mental clutter. Thoughts are habitual, so to change them, you must figure out which of the cognitive distortions you read in chapter one you struggle with the most and replace it with a healthier thought choice. However, it's not just excessive worrying and overthinking that contribute to your mental clutter—it's the life you are leading too. Do you sleep in late? Do you eat healthily? Are you getting enough exercise? Are you spending too much time on technology? Is the company you keep supportive? Are there any negative influences in your life? These are all contributors to your mental clutter, and to change them, you must develop and stick to different habits. The following are some ways of beating your old habits and maintaining new ones.[71]

---

[71] Chua, C. (n.d.). *6 Proven Ways to Make New Habits Stick.* [online] Available at: https://www.lifehack.org/articles/featured/6-proven-ways-to-make-new-habits-stick.html

Determine Why Your New Habit Doesn't Stick

As previously mentioned, one reason your old habit appeared again is because of your history. Whatever new habit you are trying to replace your old patterns with, find the trigger and challenge it. For example, if one of your habits you want to change is to wake up earlier, figure out why you keep waking up late to begin with. Is it because you go to sleep late? Is it because your thoughts keep you up at night? Try creating a sleep schedule to prepare for bed. This schedule may consist of:

- Taking a hot bath an hour before your set bedtime.
- Eating a light snack thirty minutes before you want to wind down.
- Not spending most of your time in the bedroom during the day (as this can tell your

body that your bedroom is where you *stay awake* and not *sleep*).

- Removing technology and screen time fifteen minutes before relaxing.
- Setting your alarm for the time you want to wake up.
- Meditating.

What you need to realize is that all of your habits *trigger a reaction*. If you had a different schedule before you went to sleep, doing just *one* of those things will trigger your old habit. Some examples include playing on your phone before brushing your teeth, or eating a full course meal before laying down; avoid these old habits so that your new one can be successful.

Group Same Habits Together

If you want to change your negative thinking patterns, you must figure out what triggers them to happen. For example, if you are used to overthinking because of a specific feeling, find healthier ways to deal with that feeling and maybe do some research about that feeling. If you are angry and anger triggers your thoughts to think poorly of your surroundings and people around you, then find out *why*. Maybe someone said something to tick you off, which made you feel angry and caused your thoughts to explode and clutter your mind. Instead of letting this happen, find out why the person said what they said, then ask yourself questions about what you can do to make yourself not stress over it. Just because someone thinks you are in the wrong doesn't make it a fact—it makes it an *opinion*. Grouping past habits together can help you replace the triggers and links to your previous habits to make healthier ones.

Plan, Schedule, and Track Your Habits

Being disorganized is one of the primary problems for mental clutter and results in old habits breaking through.[72] Put together a schedule for what you wish to obtain and tackle each one daily until you have completed your set habitual list. This schedule could look like:

- Wake up, make a smoothie, go for a morning jog.
- Shower, have a light snack, check social media for twenty minutes.
- Do something important, such as grocery shopping, planning dinner, scheduling what to do at work, or cleaning the house.
- Pick up your kids from school
- Make dinner

Plan and prioritize what you would like done and attempt to do one thing healthy towards decluttering your mind every day. When you plan your schedule, make sure you take into account how long each task takes. If you weren't

---

[72] Mansfield, B. (2018). The Link Between Clutter & Stress (How to Declutter). [online] Available at: https://www.yourmodernfamily.com/clutter-causes-stress/

able to get everything done on that day, maybe make a task list before you go to sleep. Before moving onto the next habit you would like to accomplish, leave yourself a five-minute mental preparation period to transition yourself to the next task.

It takes about 90 days to make a habit[73], so it's best to track your scheduled habits. Look in your calendar every day for three months, and every day that you have completed your daily habit successfully, checkmark the box. Every day that you don't mark an X, and every day that you half did your new pattern, make a slash (/).

Involve Other People

Do you have a friend or family member that lives close to the same life as you do? Do you think you could commit them to change as well?

---

[73] Gates, D. (n.d.). *Why Old Habits Die Hard!* [online] Available at: https://bodyecology.com/articles/why-old-habits-die-hard/

Round up your friends and have them join in on your daily habitual planning. New patterns are always more successful if you have someone to encourage and support you along the way. For example, you will have days where you don't want to do anything, but if you have someone doing it with you, they can motivate you out of that mindset and continue.

For the rest of this chapter, we will tackle everything discussed in this book as a care aid for when you fall off track. Think of this as your go-to when you fail or when you need a refresher about what to do when you overthink. This last chapter is about helping you figure out how to develop new habits and get back on track when you make a mistake.

Immediate Ways to Kill Stress[74]

Stress can come in multiple forms, whether it is work, personal relationships, or an overflowing inbox of emails and tasks to do. It is not about how busy your life gets or how overworked you feel; it is more about how you balance and think about the choices you make leading up to these stressors. If life becomes too much and you feel as though there is overwhelming pressure, the best thing to do is to take a step back, breathe, and get refocused on your goal. These next few steps should help you overcome stress and get centered and back to finding and living a decluttered mentality.

Snap Back to Reality

"I will look bad in front of my boss."

---

[74] Simon, J. (2013). *Kill Stress in Five Minutes or Less*. [online] Available at https://medium.com/texas-mccombs/kill-stress-in-five-minutes-or-less-1985df4b6f08

"What if my partner thinks I am not doing enough?"

"How am I ever going to meet this deadline?"

"I must do my best, or these bills will get out of hand."

Stop. Amid the struggle, we see more negative and overthink the worst until we are spiraling out of control. If you have learned anything in the first few chapters of this book, it's that thinking this way only promotes more stress, which increases mental clutter. Snap out of it—think before you hit send on an angry message, meditate before you go into that important meeting, and breathe before you snap on your partner for something they didn't do. Take a step back and question your thoughts. What got you to this point? What will help? How can you release your tension healthily?

Ground Yourself in the Present Moment

Remember the chapter on meditation and mindfulness? During overwhelming stress and deadlines, take a five-minute break to just meditate. Do you have a favorite mantra that can calm you instantly? Now is the time to use it. If you have to use the excuse to go outside for some air, or if you need to use the washroom to take a little grounding moment, do so. Remember the steps, close your eyes, take a big breath or a sigh of relief and pay attention to what's going on around and inside of you.

- What can you hear?
- What do you see?
- What can you touch? What does it feel like?
- What is your body doing?
- What can you smell?

Bring your attention to the here and now as if nothing else matters. Your demanding boss can wait, your disagreement with your spouse can wait, and your children can wait. All the matters is you at this moment. When you take a moment to bring yourself back to the present, you can go into whatever is stressing you out and tackle it calmly and with a clearer perspective.

Confide in Someone

As you have learned in chapter seven, toxic people are all around you. Hopefully, you have taken steps to identify who these people are and rid them from your inner-circle. When you are overwhelmed, it can help to talk to someone you trust—someone who supports you and brings you up. Is there anyone that comes to mind? Try calling them or scheduling a lunch date. If the problem is with your boss, don't waste your time and energy talking to your coworkers, as this creates drama that you don't need—go directly to your boss. If your stress is coming from a spouse or friend, confide in someone who supports you but not someone close to both of you as it's easy to have them get involved. If your stress is because of a decision you made that you are now regretting, take a moment to confide in your journal and read over it when you are done to gain a different perspective.

Combatting stress is all about figuring out where it's coming from then coping with it at the moment. Once you have calmed down, return to the moment. Always pat yourself on the back once you have accomplished this as it teaches your brain how to do it automatically. After your busy day, remember to be your own best friend. With any other stressors that have been itching to surface, take some time to write out and think about them. Decrease each one and don't make excuses for why you cannot because you are too busy. Not paying attention to stress and overcoming it little by little is like not learning how to challenge your inner critic. The voices get louder, and the pile of stress keeps building and building. Only you have the power to control your life and your thoughts.

Words of Affirmation Can Heal The Soul[75]

One reason you sought this book was most likely because you were struggling with overthinking and constant negativity, which led to excessive pressure and mental clutter. In this book, you learned that positivity is the aid in overcoming your inner critic and decluttering your mind. We all have off days and we all experience weaknesses from time to time, and we cannot seem to stray from our negative thought patterns; however, in these moments, what we look for the most is positivity. When you struggle to find positivity, what better time is there to

---

[75] Hurst, K. (2018). *5 Powerful Affirmations for Happiness and Instant Positivity.* [online] Available at: http://www.thelawofattraction.com/5-powerful-affirmations-for-happiness-now/

open up your gratitude journal and reread your notes? What better time to break out of the slump? The following list comprises five positive **affirmations** you can use at any moment of your life.

"I am enough."

Often when we are down, we don't feel good enough. Our old habits break through and we battle with our inner critic justifying our failures. When you tell yourself that you are enough, you give yourself the love that no one else has to give you. All the life pressures and internal insecurities don't seem as bad because you truly *are* enough.

"I have everything I need to be successful and optimistic right now."

When you think about it, what do you really need? We need love, guidance, protection, security, happiness, and the confidence that only *we* can give to ourselves. Trust that you have everything you need right now to be successful. All the elements of being human are with you at this moment. Even if the world seems like it's at a dark place, trust that it will get better because *you* will make it better. You have everything you need right now to make the choices to stay positive.

"I will follow my dreams because I am a confident individual."

Did you grow up with older peers expecting too much from you? Were you bullied and given too much pressure? Did someone you love tell you you would never make it? Forget everything that has brought you to this very moment and remember all that you have ever done for yourself. Close your eyes for a moment and rid your life of everyone that has ever been an influence on you and center your focus to yourself. What have you strived to do for not just yourself but for others too? What are your hopes, dreams, and desires? Is it a fact that what someone else has said will come true? What you do in this very second to count for your future dreams and goals is the fact. Hold on to that phrase and be confident that you will follow your dreams because that is what you deserve.

"I have the power, and no one can take that away from me."

You are always in control of your thoughts, feelings, and actions. As mentioned previously, your thoughts do not define who you are or what you do with your feelings. Your behaviors may portray an attitude that people may or may not judge. By allowing someone to take advantage of you and bring you down or make you second-guess your internal instincts, you give them power. In reality though, are you really? No one can force you to think, feel, or act, as you have the power to determine your own beliefs and values.

"My future is my choice, and my choice is happiness."

This one is my favorite because it's true that everyone has a choice; although not everyone makes the choice to be happy, it takes an awareness of this decision to make it a reality. What has sadness, anger, and disappointment ever done for you? What have you gained from being unhappy? Ask about the things that have happened because of your conscious choice to be joyful When you can know the difference in happiness, sadness, and anger, you will see the many things that have unfolded for you by making the choice towards contentment.

Optimism is not what you do; it's what you think. Pessimism is not how you act, but how you think. These five affirmations can attract positivity in any circumstance in your life. They are also great replacement thoughts for when your inner critic becomes too loud. Part of becoming more optimistic on the spot comes with the confidence of belief that you are worthy and loved.

Confidence Boosting Techniques[76]

There are many things that hold us back in life, whether it be toxic people, overwhelming stress, the need to fit in, or loneliness. However, a lack of confidence should never be one of them. So many people struggle with confidence because they believe so much of what others say and follow the image of what society expects us to be. With that, it's no wonder that confidence is hard to reach. Self-recognition and confidence cannot be achieved overnight, but we can work on it and allow it to develop more over time. Here are

---

[76] Paudyl, N. (2019). *9 Exercises You Should Practice Every Day to Boost Your Confidence*. [online] Available at:
https://www.lifehack.org/articles/productivity/9-exercises-you-should-practice-every-day-boost-your-confidence.html

some things you can do every day to boost your confidence.

Implement a Well-Balanced Diet

It is said that *you are what you eat.* To make more sense of this statement, it means that if you feed yourself junk, you will also *feel* like junk. If you consume a healthy diet, you will feel healthy. A large range of mental illnesses stems from what we feed ourselves as excess sugar and unhealthy nutrition get digested in our gut. Have you ever heard of **the gut-brain connection**? Your brain is directly connected to your gut, and what you feed yourself goes into your gut, which affects the way you think and feel. And, as mentioned, how we think and feel directly influences how we act.

Exercise Often

Whether it be yoga, stretching, standing and working, crunches, squats, running, or whatever else that comes to mind, exercise is a necessary component to confidence. Getting your blood flowing and gaining oxygen to important muscle groups in your body promotes *serotonin hormone release*, making you feel good. When your muscles aren't moving or you are constantly sitting around, our human instinct of productivity decreases, which can make us feel sluggish and depressed. Confidence stems from being proud of yourself and feeling good about the things you do. So when you see results with your body, you will feel it in your mind too.

Challenge That Inner Critic[77]

We will always come back to this one because it is *so* important. How can anyone be confident

---

[77] Desy, P. (2019). *Three Causes of Mental Clutter*. [online] Available at: https://www.learnreligions.com/causes-of-mental-clutter-1729494

when their mind constantly plays tricks on them? When the inner critic gets too loud, listen to it and ask it where it's coming from. Is there something that triggered the thought? Are you living in the here and now? Is there something you have been avoiding? What is causing the inner critic to speak up? Overthinking leads to unhealthy habits which lead to more unhelpful thoughts. Figure out if there is anything you can do to change the way you are thinking and feeling. If there is not, bring your attention to what's going on right now. Later when you are calmer, make a list of all your fears and worries, then go through each one and come up with solutions. This will help boost your confidence and change your mental state.

Live in the Moment—All the Time

Similar to combatting your inner critic, bringing yourself to this moment is another technique to boost confidence and individuality. While it may be difficult, remember the practice of being mindful and pay attention to what's happening for you right now. The past is something you can learn from, and the future is still untold. Even through your best efforts to solve upcoming problems, you will never truly make a wise choice until the situation is sitting right in front of you. Sometimes, it's best to just sit and do nothing or sleep on it until you have a clear state of mind to think about your problems. Obsessing over every negative thought or perspective will only trigger more negative outlooks, not helping to promote confidence. Try living every moment in the present and focusing on the now. You and those around you will thank you for it, ultimately making you feel better and more self-assured.

Stay True to Who You Are

Confidence is about being okay with you are and being comfortable in your own skin. Through the lessons in this book, it may take some time to feel this way, but the best strategy to practice it is to love yourself for everything that you are. Staying true to yourself is the most attractive thing anyone can do for themselves and part of the process is to believe in yourself and trust your instincts. If something doesn't feel right, go against it. If something feels off, don't question it. If you feel your morals and boundaries are being questioned, listen to what you feel deep down and make the right decision. Even if you make a mistake, failure is part of being human. When you stick to your true self, confidence will come easy.

As briefly mentioned, confidence cannot happen in the blink of an eye because it takes practice to feel confident. By taking care of yourself, making efforts towards healthier habits, and striving towards your full potential in everything you do, you develop confidence. So, what makes the difference between living your life and living a *confident* life? It is your attitude and the intention behind everything you do. If you believe you can, then you will achieve greatness—be *confident* in that.

Get Rid of Digital Clutter—You Don't Need It

We talked about this in a previous chapter—we all know how distracting technology can be. When we try to work, our phones or our smartwatches can get in the way. Sometimes we think a notification is important, only for it to just be something we subscribed to a long time ago. There are also times when you are in a heated argument and take a break just to get notified for a promoting offer. Or, when we are researching trying to gain some perspective for our own personal growth, and we get distracted by a notification saying there are cookies that we have to accept and our computer system is crashing. With the endless updates of apps on our devices or the ongoing social feeds and posts we follow—*it never ends!* We call this **digital clutter**. As much as it doesn't seem like a pain, it can really take over your life if you aren't careful. Digital clutter adds to mental clutter, which then adds to more unhealthy habits and down spiraling worries. The following is a list of things you can do to help alleviate your digital stress. [78]

Unsubscribe From Unimportant News

Any subscription service you no longer read is now unimportant digital clutter. There may have been a time when you were interested in soccer or crochet because of something you read. To continue reading and learning about it, you had to subscribe to get all the latest updates. Over time, your interests have changed, yet there is still a long list of subscriptions tied to you.

---

[78] Singleton, C. (2019). *Digital Declutter — 15 Ways to Become More Productive and Less Distracted in 2019*. [online] Available at https://www.stylefactoryproductions.com/blog/declutter-your-digital-life

Another unimportant subscription is when you first signed up to Facebook, Twitter, or any other social feed site and they automatically add you in their emails. Often, these emails can become annoying and distracting, so unsubscribing is the best policy.

Take Charge of Your Inbox

It isn't enough to go through your mail and delete emails, or even getting rid of them for good in the delete folder. If you want to clear out your inbox entirely, do it the right way. Group emails by their senders so you can easily see who is sending what and how much, rather than having a long and daunting list of individual emails to go through. Create folders for important notices and then have your mail go directly to their designated spots through your settings, or however your email provider is set up.

Organize and Declutter Your Inbox

Is your desktop an unorganized, cluttered, visual mess with shortcuts flying everywhere? Is your whole screen filled up by things you have put aside, PDF files that have no homes, and updates automatically creating shortcuts from your installments? The first thing to do is scan over every desktop app and shortcut and move it to the recycle bin. When you are down to the most important ones you want to keep, move them to somewhere else easily accessible on your computer. Once you have officially done that, delete all the contents in your recycle bin so it doesn't weigh in on your mind that you removed the wrong application. No second-guessing with this one.

Go Through Your Apps and Uninstall the Ones You Don't Use

Apps are everywhere on your computer, your smart devices, among other electronics. Go through every device and delete what you aren't using anymore. Not only will this free up space electronically, but mentally as well.

Delete Your Downloads

You can delete everything in your downloads folder without disrupting the other systems on your computer. If it's important, more than likely it will be somewhere else, like in a game you downloaded or in your pictures. Your download folder is just a reminder of what you downloaded previously and so that new downloads have a place to go. A good strategy is to delete the contents in this folder monthly.

Turn off Distracting Notifications

You can turn your notifications off in the settings of your digital devices, similar to unsubscribing to emails. Do this so you won't receive any unimportant notifications.

Take a Look at Your Web Browser

Your web browser is possibly the worst of your mental and digital clutter because it is always hidden. First, look at your browsing history and remove any unimportant data. Then, delete and clear your cache and all your cookies. Finally, remove any plugins or extensions that you are no longer using. This will speed up your web browser and make for a faster research experience. You may need to look up more about how to delete your cache and clear your cookies depending on the browser you are using.

Limit Your Screen Time

Many people struggle with this one because technology and digital devices have become addictive in our society. We always want to know what's happening in the world with our followers and the people we follow. We want to keep up to date so we don't miss out; or if we are a promoter or marketer, we try to keep up with the latest fashions and deals. The worst time to be in front of our screens is as soon as we wake up and right before we go to bed. The easiest way to cut down on your screen time is by installing a *screen time app* so it can monitor your usage. After a week, you should gain some insight on how much screen time you use and start making goals to decrease it by about 10% every week.

That's it. From killing stress to promoting positivity, defeating your inner critic, and letting go of more than just mental clutter, this chapter has it all. Digital clutter can drag people down and leave them feeling like there are more tasks to do than there really is. With believing as though there is too much pressure and stress, the last thing you need is to be brought down from too much technology and distractions.

Final Words

Think back to the person you were when you picked up this book. Are you still that same person now after finishing it? Probably, but do you finally know what to do to be the best version of yourself? Also probably. When you really take into account everything that our brains are responsible for, it's safe to say that it's pretty amazing. Your brain is a part of you, which makes you pretty amazing too. I hope that after finishing this book, you aren't afraid to be yourself, take care of yourself, and truly love yourself because that is all it takes to declutter the mind.

With every chapter you have read, you can figure out which one was the most important to you and why. Which message spoke the clearest? Was it how to be confident and love yourself fully? Or was it the different negative cognitive distortions that take place in your mind when you are battling your inner critic? Whatever it is, it's safe to say that you have more information now than you did when you first read this book. This should give you more clarity and perspective. Your job now is to figure out what is still bugging you. What is still eating your mind that you can't get through, and how can you use this book as a tool to guide you towards opportunity and success?

When you think about your future, where do you see yourself in five years? Where do you see yourself in ten years? Part of getting out of the mental rut you are in is envisioning where you are headed and then make goals and change habits to get yourself there. Think about the relationships in your life and determine which friends and family members are here to support you. Think about your career and figure out if they make you happy. If you are not happy, ask yourself what else you could do to help you feel better about yourself. Life is an emotional and mental rollercoaster, but it doesn't have to be if you clear your mind and look for opportunities right in front of you.

In the introduction, I promised you would learn how to declutter your mind so you could be the best version of yourself. Hopefully, through the steps outlined in this book, you can see through the lies your mind traps you in so you can bring your best self to the table. The solution is simple; if digital clutter distracts you, diminish it. If toxic people surround you, decrease contact with them. If you struggle with confidence, give yourself time and patience to get there. If you lead a busy life, change it. Many people will make excuses for change because they are afraid of it. However, the choice was yours in the beginning, it's yours now, and it will still be yours, years from this moment - you can let fear control you, or you can use it to grow and flourish through life.

In chapter one, you learned that procrastination and avoidance can increase mental clutter. You read that the past, present, and future can all play a major role in why you feel so tied down. In chapter four, you learned that the only way to live in the present moment is to practice meditation. Chapter one explained the negative thinking patterns, and chapter five helped you define the inner critical voice and taught you how to challenge those thoughts. In chapter two, you learned the heaviness that stress can weigh on your mind and your physical wellbeing. This chapter was perhaps the most important chapter to pay attention to when defining what causes your mental clutter, as stress is the one thing that is the hardest to escape from. To go further, chapter seven outlined **tools and techniques**

to use to decrease your unhealthy stress and anxiety.

Sometimes, all it takes is for you to count backward from ten or go for a brisk walk to clear your mind. Chapter three explained **the myth behind why you feel so busy**, which is why you feel as though you have no time to yourself. However, taking time for yourself, as you have learned, is crucial to inner peace and happiness. When you look at your schedule, you may see that it is busy but there is always some time right before you go to sleep to give yourself some much-needed love. Even with your best efforts in decluttering your busy and stressed mind, your relationships can play a huge role in bringing you down—just when you feel you are doing better. In chapter six, you learned about **how to identify these toxic people** and what a healthy relationship looks like. If you have honesty, trust, respect, and independence in your personal life, it will come naturally to hold this power, sharing your life with anyone else. Don't forget **effective communication skills** that chapter six has explained to you as well.

If you were to take anything from this book and use it in your daily life, I would ask that you bookmark one chapter and live by its rules and structure. All the information inside this book that was provided to you was information to help you understand mental clutter. The last four chapters gave you strategies to use in your everyday life. For me, learning about toxicity and the people I surrounded myself with were things I needed to continue to live by. Being an empathetic person, I always believed the best in people. Such is not a curse, nor is it necessarily a blessing either; however, I love people and having supportive ones by my side through thick and thin, which is what helps me stay at peace. A take-home message from me is to just be yourself in every aspect of your life. Don't be a follower, don't succumb to what society expects of you. Just be you and do it unapologetically.

Cheers.

Resources

Best, J. (2018). Mental Clutter. *Association of Professional Declutterers and Organisers*. Retrieved from https://www.apdo.co.uk/mental-clutter/

Bradberry, T. (2015). 5 ways to organize your mind for maximum productivity. *World Economic Forum*. Retrieved from https://www.weforum.org/agenda/2015/11/5-ways-to-organize-your-mind-for-maximum-productivity/

Brock, F. (2019). The single principle you need to clean out the mind clutter for good. *Becoming Minimalist*. Retrieved from https://www.becomingminimalist.com/declutter-your-mind/

Burkeman, O. (2016). Why you feel busy all the time (when you're actually not). *BBC*. Retrieved from http://www.bbc.com/future/story/20160909-why-you-feel-busy-all-the-time-when-youre-actually-not

Cherry, K. (2019). Understanding the psychology of positive thinking. *Verywell Mind*. Retrieved from https://www.verywellmind.com/what-is-positive-thinking-2794772

Chen, W. (2016). How to rewire your brain for positivity and happiness. *Buffer*. Retrieved from https://buffer.com/resources/how-to-rewire-your-brains-for-positivity-and-happiness

Chua, C. (n.d.). 6 proven ways to make new habits stick. *Lifehack*. Retrieved from https://www.lifehack.org/articles/featured/6-proven-ways-to-make-new-habits-stick.html

Craig, H. (2019). 10 ways to build trust in a relationship. *Positive Psychology*. Retrieved from https://positivepsychology.com/build-trust/

Cummings, H. (2017). The effect of social media on the brain. *Collegiate Times*. Retrieved from http://www.collegiatetimes.com/lifestyles/the-effect-of-social-media-on-the-brain/article_f27b5a1e-b999-11e7-bfc2-77d77ccdf0b1.html

Desy, P. I. (2019). Three causes of mental clutter. *Learn Religions*. Retrieved from https://www.learnreligions.com/causes-of-mental-clutter-1729494

Dowling, D. (n.d.). 4 ways to be your own best friend. *Mind Body Green*. Retrieved from https://www.mindbodygreen.com/0-15298/4-ways-to-be-your-own-best-friend.html

Gates, D. (n.d.). Why old habits die hard! *Body Ecology*. Retrieved from https://bodyecology.com/articles/why-old-habits-die-hard/

Goodlet, N. (n.d.). 5 ways to become your own best friend. *Lifehack*. Retrieved from https://www.lifehack.org/articles/lifestyle/5-ways-become-your-own-best-friend.html

Hurst, K. (2018). 5 powerful affirmations for happiness and instant positivity. *The Law of Attraction*. Retrieved from http://www.thelawofattraction.com/5-powerful-affirmations-for-happiness-now/

Inner IDEA. (n.d.). Meditation 101: Techniques, benefits, and a beginner's how-to. *Gaiam*. Retrieved from https://www.gaiam.com/blogs/discover/meditation-101-techniques-benefits-and-a-beginner-s-how-to

Kenison, K. (2000). Why you must have time alone. *Oprah*. Retrieved from http://www.oprah.com/spirit/why-you-must-have-solitude-and-time-for-yourself/all

Klein, S. (2013). Adrenaline, cortisol, norepinephrine: The three major stress hormones, explained. *Huffington Post*. Retrieved from https://www.huffingtonpost.ca/2013/04/19/adrenaline-cortisol-stress-hormones_n_3112800.html

Mansfield, B. (2018). The link between clutter & stress (How to declutter): Clutter causes stress. *Your Modern Family*. Retrieved from https://www.yourmodernfamily.com/clutter-causes-stress/

McGauran, D. (2019). 7 ways to re-frame your thinking. *ActiveBeat*. Retrieved from https://www.activebeat.com/your-health/women/7-ways-to-re-frame-your-thinking/?streamview=all

McGauran, D. (2015). 12 negative thought patterns that play havoc in life. *ActiveBeat*. Retrieved from https://www.activebeat.com/your-health/12-negative-thought-patterns-that-play-havoc-in-life/12/

Morin, A. (2019). How cognitive reframing is used in mental health. *Verywell Mind*. Retrieved from https://www.verywellmind.com/reframing-defined-2610419

Morin, A. (2016). This is how your thoughts become your reality. *Forbes*. Retrieved from https://www.forbes.com/sites/amymorin/2016/06/15/this-is-how-your-thoughts-become-your-reality/#7e672492528a

Morin, A. (2019). 10 simple ways to always think positive thoughts. *Lifehack*. Retrieved from https://www.lifehack.org/articles/communication/10-tips-make-positive-thinking-easy.html

Nazish, N. (2018). How to overcome mental fatigue, according to an expert. *Forbes*. Retrieved from https://www.forbes.com/sites/nomanazish/2018/09/25/how-to-overcome-mental-fatigue-according-to-an-expert/#1159fd621644

Neustaeter, B. (2016). 10 things that hold more importance in a relationship than love. *Narcity*. Retrieved from https://www.narcity.com/ca/on/toronto/dating/10-things-that-are-actually-more-important-in-a-relationship-than-love

Nicholas, R. (2017). How do my thoughts impact my life? *Charis Counseling Center*. Retrieved from https://www.chariscounselingcenter.com/blog/how-do-my-thoughts-impact-my-life/

Oppong, T. (2017). The mindset advantage: How your mental frame affects your behavior and performance. *Medium*. Retrieved from https://medium.com/the-mission/the-mindset-advantage-how-your-mental-frame-affects-your-behavior-and-performance-1b08aa4c2d97

Paudyl, N. (2014). 9 exercises you should practice every day to boost your confidence. *Lifehack*. Retrieved from https://www.lifehack.org/articles/productivity/9-exercises-you-should-practice-every-day-boost-your-confidence.html

Scott, E. (2019). How your stress response is triggered. *Verywell Mind*. Retrieved from https://www.verywellmind.com/what-is-a-stress-response-3145148

Segal, J., Smith, M., Segal, R., & Robinson, L. (2019). Stress symptoms signs and causes. *HelpGuide*. Retrieved from https://www.helpguide.org/articles/stress/stress-symptoms-signs-and-causes.htm

Simon, J. (2013). Kill stress in five minutes or less. *Medium*. Retrieved from https://medium.com/texas-mccombs/kill-stress-in-five-minutes-or-less-1985df4b6f08

Singleton, C. (2019). Digital declutter — 15 ways to become more productive and less distracted in 2019.

Style Factory. Retrieved from https://www.stylefactoryproductions.com/blog/declutter-your-digital-life

Smith, E.-M. (n.d.). What is negative thinking? How it destroys your mental health. *Healthy Place*. Retrieved from https://www.healthyplace.com/self-help/positivity/what-is-negative-thinking-how-it-destroys-your-mental-health

SoP. (2016). The limbic system. *The Science of Psychotherapy*. Retrieved from https://www.thescienceofpsychotherapy.com/the-limbic-system/

Stevenson, A. (2019). Everyday habits that zap your energy and make you feel sluggish. *Health Prep*. Retrieved from https://healthprep.com/living-healthy/8-everyday-habits-that-zap-your-energy-and-make-you-feel-sluggish/2/?utm_source=google&utm_campaign=1698316511&utm_medium=search&utm_term=overwhelming%20exhaustion&utm_content=66177941437

What is Dissociation and What to Do About It? (2012). *WA State CBT+*. Retrieved from https://depts.washington.edu/hcsats/PDF/TF-%20CBT/pages/7%20Trauma%20Focused%20CBT/Dissociation-Information.pdf

7 Types of Toxic People and How to Spot Them. (n.d.). *Science of People*. Retrieved from https://www.scienceofpeople.com/toxic-people/